iPad Seniors Guide

Navigating the Digital Age with Confidence – A
Comprehensive Step-by-Step, Illustrated Guide for
Seniors to Master iPad Features, Communication,
and Entertainment

Elliot Ravensdale

Table of Content

Chapter 1. Introduction to iPad for Seniors

Embark on an enlightening journey with your iPad, a marvel of modern technology that blends sophistication with ease of use. Here, you'll be guided through the essentials of navigating and appreciating this remarkable device. Designed with your needs in mind, these pages are more than just a guide; they are a gateway to rediscovering the world around you. The iPad is not merely a gadget; it's a companion that resonates with your lifestyle. It promises simplicity in its operation and depth in its potential.

Welcome to the World of iPad

Welcome to the exciting journey of discovering the iPad, a device that has revolutionized the way we interact with technology. As you embark on this new adventure, imagine holding a window to the world, one that responds to your touch, brings you closer to your loved ones, and opens up a universe of information and entertainment.

The iPad, sleek and intuitive, is more than just a gadget; it's a companion for your curiosity and a tool for your everyday needs. Unlike the bulky computers of the past or the tiny screens of smartphones, the iPad strikes a perfect balance with its generous screen and portable design. It's like having a personal canvas that adjusts to your desires – be it reading, watching, learning, or simply exploring.

For those who are just stepping into the realm of tablets, the iPad can seem daunting at first. It's natural to feel a bit of tech anxiety, but remember, every expert was once a beginner. The key lies in embracing the experience with an open mind. Think of the iPad as a friendly guide, eager to help you navigate this new digital landscape.

The heart of the iPad experience lies in its touch interface. Gone are the days of cumbersome keyboards and unresponsive buttons. Your iPad responds to the simplest of gestures – a tap, a swipe, a pinch. It's like learning a new language, one that's surprisingly intuitive. Imagine flipping through pages of a book, or gliding through photographs with just a flick of your finger. That's the magic of the iPad – it conforms to the most natural of human motions.

Understanding your iPad starts with its basic layout. The screen, a vibrant display of icons and apps, is your gateway to endless possibilities. Each icon is a door, behind which lies tools and games, news and stories, connections and memories. The simplicity of the layout belies its potential – with each tap, you're not just opening an app; you're unlocking new experiences.

One of the first things you'll notice is the Dock, a customizable space at the bottom of the screen. Think of it as your personal toolbox, where you can keep your most-used apps. Whether it's the photo album that holds your cherished memories, or the note-taking app where you jot down your thoughts, the Dock keeps what's important at your fingertips.

As you explore your iPad, you'll encounter the Control Center – a handy feature that gives you quick access to essential tools. With a swipe and a tap, you can adjust the brightness, turn on the flashlight, or set a timer. It's like having a command center that's tailored to your needs.

One of the most delightful aspects of using an iPad is the ease with which you can connect with others. With apps like FaceTime and Messages, distance becomes irrelevant. Picture seeing your grandchild's face and sharing a laugh, as if they were right there with you. The iPad bridges miles and brings hearts closer, making every interaction a joyous occasion.

Now, let's address a common concern – tech anxiety. It's perfectly normal to feel overwhelmed by something new, but the iPad is designed with you in mind. Its interface is clean and uncluttered, its instructions clear, and its operations forgiving. Mistakes are just steps in the learning process, and with each use, you'll find your confidence growing.

As you continue on this path, remember that the iPad is more than a device; it's a gateway to learning, a bridge to loved ones, and a canvas for your passions. Embrace this journey with enthusiasm and patience, and you'll discover that the world of iPad is a world of wonder waiting for you.

Understanding Your iPad: Basic Concepts

Embarking on the journey with your new iPad, you are not just holding a piece of technology; you are holding a key to a new world of experiences and knowledge.

At its core, the iPad is a marvel of simplicity. Its design speaks of an intuitive understanding of human interaction with technology. The sleek, minimalistic exterior belies the complexity of the world it contains. It's like opening a book to find not just words but a universe of stories, each waiting to be explored.

The most striking aspect of the iPad is its display. Bright, clear, and vibrant, the screen is your window into everything the iPad offers. Unlike the bulky televisions or the small, cramped screens of older phones, the iPad's screen is the perfect canvas for your digital explorations. It's large enough to enjoy videos or read comfortably, yet compact enough to carry around with ease.

Navigating this digital canvas is achieved through touch — a language that is both ancient and modern. Your fingers become the conduits of your commands. Swipe through pages like a book, tap to select, pinch to zoom in or out. It's a dance of gestures, each as intuitive as turning a page or pointing at something of interest.

Understanding the iPad also means getting acquainted with its brain – the operating system, iOS. Think of it as the director of a play, ensuring every actor and scene comes together seamlessly. iOS is what makes your iPad not just a screen, but a smart, responsive device that anticipates and reacts to your needs. With each update, iOS evolves, learning new tricks to make your life easier and your iPad experience more enjoyable.

One of the gems of using an iPad is its App Store, a treasure trove of applications. Imagine a library where, instead of books, there are apps for everything you can think of – from keeping track of your health to learning a new language, from connecting with friends to playing games that sharpen your mind. Each app is a new adventure, a new tool, a new way to enhance your life.

Your iPad also serves as a bridge to the world through the internet. With Safari, the built-in web browser, the global village is at your fingertips. Search for information, watch videos from across the world, or shop from the comfort of your home. The web is vast, and your iPad is your vessel to navigate its endless waters.

Let's talk about communication. Your iPad is not just a device; it's a portal to connect with family and friends. Through messaging apps, emails, or video calls, your iPad helps shrink distances and bring your loved ones closer. Imagine seeing your family's faces, sharing stories, and creating memories, all through the screen of your iPad.

Now, addressing the elephant in the room – tech anxiety. It's normal to feel overwhelmed when faced with something new. But remember, the iPad was designed with all users in mind. Its user interface is intuitive, guiding you gently through each process. Mistakes? They are just part of the learning curve, and with the iPad, they are easy to correct.

As you continue this journey, remember that understanding your iPad is like getting to know a new friend. There's a period of learning and adaptation, but with time, it becomes a trusted companion. Your iPad is a gateway to a world of possibilities, and with each tap, swipe, and pinch, you are not just using a device; you are embracing a new way of engaging with the world.

Overcoming Tech Anxiety: A Guide for Beginners

Embarking on the journey of mastering a new technology like the iPad can often be akin to learning to navigate a new city. It's a blend of excitement and apprehension, a journey of discovery peppered with moments of uncertainty.

Tech anxiety, especially for those who didn't grow up in the digital age, is a natural response. It's the feeling of standing on the shore, looking out at the vast ocean of technology and wondering how to swim across. But remember, every journey starts with a single step, or in the case of your iPad, a single tap.

The iPad, with its sleek design and responsive touch screen, might initially feel alien. It's like holding a book for the first time, unsure of how to turn the pages. But just as you learned to read and cherish books, you will learn to navigate and love your iPad. It's not about jumping in at the deep end; it's about dipping your toes in the water and gradually acclimating to the temperature.

One of the first steps in overcoming tech anxiety is understanding that it's okay to be a beginner. Every expert in every field started as a novice. The iPad is designed to be user-friendly, with a focus on simplicity and intuition. Its interface is not a labyrinth meant to confuse but a garden path designed to be walked at your own pace.

Another key aspect is embracing the learning process. Each interaction with your iPad is an opportunity to learn. If you tap something and it doesn't do what you expected, it's not a failure; it's a learning experience. The iPad won't judge your pace or mistakes. It's a patient teacher, always ready to let you try again.

Imagine the iPad as a personal assistant, one that's ready to help but waits for your instructions. It won't rush you or push you; it's there to serve at your leisure. This mindset shift, from viewing technology as a daunting challenge to seeing it as a helpful tool, is pivotal in overcoming tech anxiety.

When you first start, focus on the basics. Learn to turn the iPad on and off. Get acquainted with swiping through the screens. Practice tapping on apps to open them and pressing the Home button to return to the starting point. These are the ABCs of your iPad journey, and like learning any new language, repetition is key.

Remember, there's no race to the finish line. Your pace is the right pace. If today you learn to send an email, that's a victory. If tomorrow you watch a video on YouTube, that's another step forward. Each small achievement is a building block in your journey of technological empowerment.

One of the most beautiful aspects of learning to use your iPad is the opportunity to connect with others. Whether it's a FaceTime call with your grandchildren or joining a community of fellow iPad users online, your iPad is a bridge to companionship and support. You're not alone in this journey; there's a whole world of learners just like you, discovering the joys of technology together.

As you continue on this path, celebrate each milestone. Did you successfully navigate to a website? That's a triumph. Did you download your first app? That's a moment of joy. Each of these accomplishments is a step away from anxiety and a step towards confidence and mastery.

In this journey of overcoming tech anxiety, remember, the iPad is not just a device; it's a portal to new experiences, a tool for personal growth, and a testament to the fact that learning and exploration are lifelong journeys. With patience, curiosity, and a sense of adventure, the world of technology is not just accessible but can become a source of joy and empowerment.

Navigating Your iPad: The Basics

Navigating your iPad is like learning the steps of a new dance. At first, the movements may feel unfamiliar, but with a little practice, you'll be moving with ease and grace. The iPad is designed to be intuitive, and this section is your guide to understanding its basic navigation, transforming potential apprehension into a delightful exploration.

The journey into the world of iPad navigation begins with the most fundamental element: the Home Screen. This is your starting point, a digital hearth from where all adventures begin. Picture it as the main hallway of a house, with each app representing a door to a different room. These rooms are where various activities and experiences take place, from chatting with loved ones to reading the latest news.

Understanding the Home Screen is akin to getting to know the layout of a new neighborhood. At first glance, it might seem like a collection of colorful squares, but each icon is a gateway to a different experience. Take time to explore these icons. Tap on them gently, like knocking on a neighbor's door, and watch as they open up new worlds for you.

The Dock, situated at the bottom of the Home Screen, is akin to your favorite tools, always within arm's reach. You can customize this area with apps you frequently use, much like placing your most beloved books on a coffee table for easy access. This customization makes your iPad feel more personal, more attuned to your daily needs.

As you become more comfortable, you'll discover the joy of swiping. Swiping is a fluid motion, a gentle glide of your finger across the screen, moving you from one page of apps to another. It's akin to browsing through pages of a photo album, each swipe revealing a new set of memories and tools.

Then there's the Control Center, a handy panel that gives you quick access to various controls and settings. Accessing it is as simple as swiping down from the top-right corner of the screen. It's like having a remote control that manages everything from your television's volume to the lights in your room. Here, you can adjust the brightness of your screen, turn on the Wi-Fi, or access the calculator. It's your command center, simplified.

One of the most endearing features of your iPad is the search function. Just swipe down from the middle of the Home Screen, and a search bar appears. It's like asking a friendly librarian to help you find a book. You type in what you're looking for, and the iPad retrieves it for you, whether it's an app, a document, or even a piece of information from the web.

Your iPad's ability to connect you with the world is one of its most powerful features. The internet browser, Safari, is your gateway to the world wide web. It's like having a magic portal that takes you to any place, any subject you wish to explore. Whether it's reading about history, watching cooking videos, or shopping online, Safari brings the world to your fingertips.

Lastly, let's talk about exiting apps and returning to the Home Screen. This action is like stepping back into the main hallway after visiting a room. On iPads with a Home button, a single press takes you back. On newer models, a short swipe up from the bottom edge of the screen does the trick. It's a simple gesture, a step back, readying you for your next adventure.

Navigating your iPad is an ongoing journey, one that gets easier and more enjoyable with each use. Like any new skill, it requires a bit of practice and patience. But the rewards are immense. With each swipe, tap, and press, you're not just moving icons around a screen; you're exploring a world of possibilities, learning new things, and connecting with others in ways you might have never imagined. Welcome to the delightful dance of navigating your iPad.

Chapter 2. Setting Up Your New iPad

Embarking on the adventure of setting up your new iPad, you are at the threshold of a world where technology meets personalization. This guide is crafted to navigate you through the initial steps, transforming your device into an extension of your own lifestyle and preferences. From the moment of unboxing to exploring the vast capabilities of your iPad, each step is an integral part of tailoring this sophisticated device to your individual needs. The journey ahead is designed to be intuitive, empowering you to take full ownership of your iPad. As you proceed, remember that your iPad is more than just a piece of technology; it's a companion that adapts and grows with you, making every interaction an enjoyable and fulfilling experience.

Unboxing and Initial Setup

Imagine a child on a crisp, sunny morning, unwrapping a gift. The anticipation, the excitement, the curiosity – this is the essence of unboxing your new iPad. As you peel away the layers of packaging, you're not just opening a box; you're unveiling a portal to new experiences. The iPad, with its sleek design and gleaming screen, sits in your hands like a canvas waiting for its first stroke of brilliance.

Your journey with the iPad begins with its first awakening. Pressing the power button, you'll witness the screen come to life, greeting you with vibrant colors and inviting you to embark on a digital adventure. This moment marks the beginning of a beautiful relationship between you and your iPad, one that promises to grow and evolve with every touch and swipe.

The initial setup of your iPad is a crucial step in molding it to become your faithful digital companion. It's a process that's been simplified to be as intuitive as the device itself. When you power on your iPad for the first time, it welcomes you with open arms, guiding you through each step with ease and clarity. The iPad's setup wizard is like a friendly tour guide, leading you through the essentials of setting up your device.

Entering your language and region is the first step in this journey. It's like telling your iPad your home address and the language you speak, so it can understand and assist you better. This customization ensures that your iPad aligns with your preferences and lifestyle from the very start.

Connecting to a Wi-Fi network is the next step. This process is akin to opening a window to the world. Your iPad, now connected to the internet, can reach out to the vast expanse of the digital universe, bringing you news, entertainment, and connections. The Wi-Fi connection is the invisible thread that ties your iPad to the tapestry of the online world.

As you proceed, your iPad will ask you to set up or log in to your Apple ID. This ID is more than just an account; it's your personal key to Apple's ecosystem. Think of it as your unique digital fingerprint, one that unlocks a world of apps, music, books, and more. With your Apple ID, your iPad becomes truly yours, holding your preferences, your downloads, and your collections.

The initial setup also introduces you to the world of customization. Your iPad offers you the freedom to choose settings that resonate with your usage and preferences. It's like arranging your room to suit your comfort and taste. From choosing a wallpaper that reflects your personality to setting up sounds that please your ears, each choice you make personalizes your iPad experience.

This setup process is more than just a series of steps; it's the beginning of a journey. With each selection and customization, you're tailoring your iPad to become an extension of yourself. It's a device that learns from you, adapts to you, and grows with you. The joy of setting up your iPad is akin to planting a seed in a garden – a seed that will grow into a tree under your care and attention, bearing fruits of knowledge, connection, and entertainment.

As you complete the setup, take a moment to admire your work. Your iPad is now ready to embark on this digital odyssey with you. It's not just a piece of technology; it's a companion, a tool, a window to the world that fits perfectly in your hands. The journey you're about to embark on with your iPad is one filled with discoveries, learning, and joy. Welcome to the world where technology meets personal touch, where every tap and swipe opens up new possibilities.

Connecting to Wi-Fi

In the journey of setting up your new iPad, connecting to Wi-Fi is akin to opening the doors to a grand library filled with endless rows of books, each brimming with knowledge, stories, and possibilities. This step is your gateway to the world, an essential bridge that links your iPad to the vast and vibrant landscape of the internet.

Imagine your iPad as a vessel, ready to set sail. The Wi-Fi connection is the water that buoys it, the current that carries it forward into the ocean of digital content. It's the invisible yet crucial link that transforms your device from a solitary island into a connected, dynamic portal to the globe.

As you initiate this connection, your iPad will present you with a list of available networks. Each network is like a different path or doorway, leading to the same expansive, digital world. Selecting your home network is the first step in this journey. It's like choosing the most familiar and comfortable route, a path you know and trust.

Entering the Wi-Fi password is the next crucial step. This process is much like turning the key in a lock, ensuring a secure and private entry into the digital realm. The password is your safeguard, a protective barrier that keeps your voyages on the internet safe and uninterrupted. As you type in these characters, you're not just inputting a code; you're fortifying your connection, ensuring your online journey is both seamless and secure.

Once connected, your iPad becomes alive with potential. It's no longer just a screen and a collection of apps; it's a window to the world. Suddenly, you have access to everything from live news feeds and weather updates to online courses and video calls with loved ones. It's like having a magic carpet that can take you anywhere, anyplace, at any time.

This Wi-Fi connection is more than just a technical necessity; it's a lifeline that keeps you tethered to the digital age. It's the thread that weaves your iPad into the fabric of your life, integrating it into your daily routine. Whether it's checking the morning news over coffee, streaming your favorite show, or video chatting with your grandchildren, the Wi-Fi connection makes it all possible.

But what if the connection falters? Just as a ship might encounter choppy waters, your journey with the iPad may sometimes hit a snag. Fear not, for troubleshooting Wi-Fi issues is often straightforward. Most problems can be solved with simple steps like checking the router, restarting your iPad, or re-entering the Wi-Fi password. It's akin to navigating through minor detours on a road trip – a temporary pause in an otherwise smooth journey.

In connecting your iPad to Wi-Fi, you're not just linking to a network; you're opening the door to exploration, learning, and connection. It's the first step in a journey that takes you beyond the physical confines of your surroundings, into a world where information, entertainment, and human connection are boundless.

As you complete this step, take a moment to marvel at the power in your hands. With your iPad now connected to Wi-Fi, the world is at your fingertips – a world that's waiting for you to explore, discover, and enjoy. The possibilities are limitless, and your journey has just begun.

Apple ID: Creating and Using It

Crafting your Apple ID is like carving out your own niche in the vast digital universe of Apple. It's a process that personalizes your iPad experience, intertwining your device with your identity, preferences, and digital lifestyle. The Apple ID is not just a username or a password; it's a key to a kingdom, a passport to a world of seamless integration across Apple's services and devices.

Imagine your Apple ID as a personal badge, one that grants you access to a realm where your photos, music, documents, and apps coexist in harmony, synced across your devices. It's the identifier that Apple uses to recognize you, ensuring that your experience is tailored and unique. Whether you're downloading an app, purchasing a book, or backing up precious memories, your Apple ID is the thread that weaves these experiences together.

Creating your Apple ID is a journey in itself. It begins with providing your basic information – an email address that becomes the cornerstone of your digital identity. This email address is like the flag you plant, claiming your space in the Apple ecosystem. Choosing a password is the next critical step. This password is akin to a secret handshake, a unique code that protects your identity and keeps your digital life secure.

But the creation of your Apple ID goes beyond just setting up login credentials. It's about laying the foundation for your experiences with your iPad. With your Apple ID, you start building your own digital library – a collection that travels with you, accessible from any of your Apple devices. It's like having a personal bookshelf that's not confined by physical space, where your favorite novels, photo albums, and records reside.

Moreover, your Apple ID is a gateway to iCloud, Apple's cloud storage service. Imagine iCloud as a safety deposit box for your digital valuables – photos, documents, contacts, and more. Everything is stored securely, updated in real-time, and accessible from any of your devices. The beauty of iCloud lies in its simplicity and efficiency; it works silently in the background, ensuring that your most cherished digital possessions are always within reach, yet safe.

But what happens if you forget your Apple ID password? Fear not, for Apple has designed recovery methods with your convenience and security in mind. It's like having a spare key to your home; even if you lose one, you're not locked out. The recovery process is straightforward, guiding you step by step to regain access to your account, ensuring that you're never stranded outside your digital home.

Using your Apple ID is an ongoing journey. It evolves with you, adapting to your changing preferences and needs. Every app you download, every purchase you make, every photo you store adds a brushstroke to the canvas of your digital life. It's a dynamic process, one that reflects your interests, your lifestyle, and your choices.

In essence, your Apple ID is more than just an account; it's an integral part of your digital identity. It's the signature you leave on every interaction with your iPad, a representation of your presence in the Apple ecosystem. As you continue to explore and enjoy your iPad, your Apple ID will be there, ensuring that every experience is personalized, every data is synced, and every moment is captured, just the way you want it.

Basic Security: Setting Up Touch ID/Face ID

In the world of technology, securing your device is akin to safeguarding a treasure chest; it's not just about protecting a piece of hardware, but also the precious data and memories it holds. The iPad offers two advanced security features – Touch ID and Face ID – that act as vigilant guardians, ensuring that your digital treasure remains secure and private.

Touch ID and Face ID are more than just security measures; they are the embodiment of a personal bond between you and your iPad. They recognize you, and only you, making your iPad as unique as a fingerprint or as distinct as the features of your face. This level of personal recognition is not just about keeping others out; it's about creating a sense of intimacy and trust with your device.

Setting up Touch ID is like teaching your iPad to recognize your touch, the unique patterns of your fingerprint. It's a simple process where you gently place your finger on the Home button, allowing the iPad to scan and memorize your fingerprint. This scan is akin to a painter capturing your essence, translating the loops and whorls of your fingerprint into a digital key that unlocks your iPad. Each time you rest your finger on the Home button, it's like a familiar handshake between you and your device, a silent acknowledgment that grants you access.

Face ID, on the other hand, takes security to a new level. It uses advanced facial recognition technology to create a detailed map of your face. Setting up Face ID is like creating a self-portrait, where the iPad uses its camera to capture and learn the unique characteristics of your face. The technology is sophisticated, yet the process is as simple as looking at your device. When you lift your iPad, it greets you, recognizes you, and unlocks itself, as if it's happy to see an old friend.

The beauty of Touch ID and Face ID lies in their perfect blend of convenience and security. Gone are the days of typing passwords or patterns. Now, accessing your iPad is as natural as looking at it or touching it. These security features are not just barriers; they are smart, intuitive gatekeepers that protect without complicating your experience.

Moreover, Touch ID and Face ID adapt to changes. Just as a friend recognizes you even if you've changed your hairstyle or grown a beard, these technologies learn and adjust to your physical changes over time. They are dynamic, evolving with you, ensuring that the security of your iPad remains constant, yet never intrusive.

But what if you need to share your iPad with a family member or a friend? Apple has thought of this too. You can register multiple fingerprints and even set up an alternate appearance for Face ID. This flexibility allows your iPad to be secure yet accessible to those you trust, much like giving a spare key to a family member.

In conclusion, setting up Touch ID and Face ID is a crucial step in your journey with the iPad. It's about more than just locking and unlocking your device; it's about creating a secure, personalized experience. These security features stand as silent sentinels, guarding your privacy and data, allowing you to enjoy the wonders of your iPad with peace of mind, knowing that your digital world is safe and secure.

Accessibility Features for Easier Use

The world of technology, particularly the realm of tablets like the iPad, is not just about advancing features and sleek designs; it's about creating a space that is inclusive and accessible to everyone. This is where the iPad's accessibility features come into play, transforming the device from a simple tablet into a versatile tool that caters to a wide range of needs and abilities. These features are not mere add-ons; they are integral components that make the iPad a device for all, breaking down barriers and opening doors to the digital world for everyone.

At the heart of the iPad's accessibility features lies a profound understanding that everyone interacts with technology differently. It acknowledges that what is intuitive for one person might be challenging for another. It's like having a personal assistant who adapts to your individual needs, ensuring that your experience with the iPad is comfortable, enjoyable, and uniquely yours.

One of the most remarkable features is VoiceOver, a screen reader designed for those who are blind or have low vision. Imagine a friend who reads out the text on the screen for you, describes every image, and even tells you about the battery level and Wi-Fi signal strength. VoiceOver does just that. It transforms the visual experience of the iPad into an auditory one, allowing you to navigate through your device with simple gestures, all the while being guided by a friendly, responsive voice.

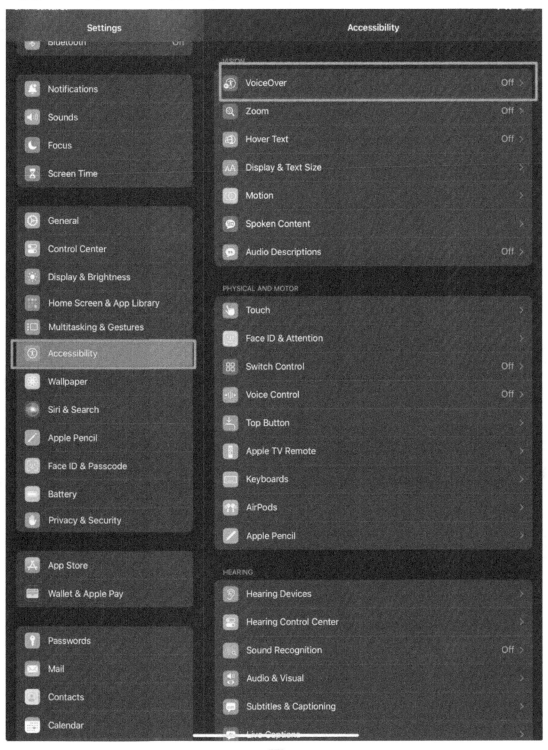

Then there's Zoom, a feature that magnifies the entire screen or just parts of it, like a digital magnifying glass. It's perfect for those who need a closer look at text, images, or even videos. Zoom follows your instructions, moving around the screen as you dictate, bringing the world within the iPad into clear view, no matter your visual capacity.

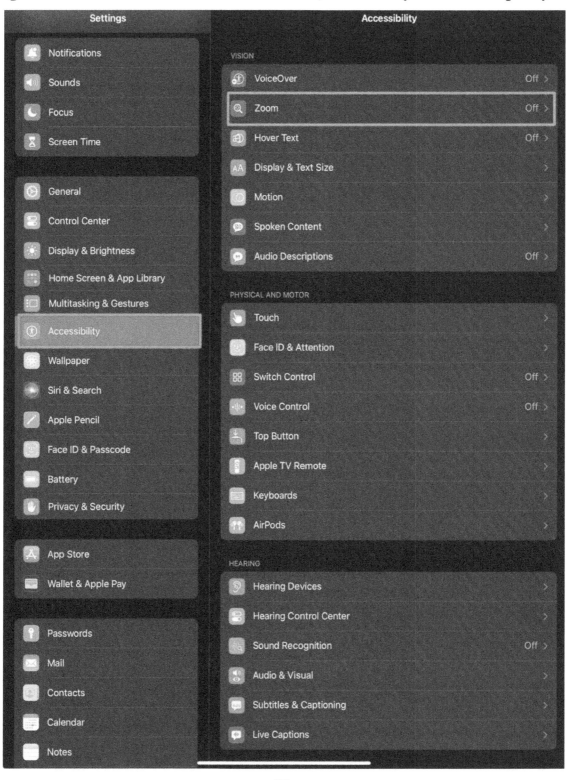

The iPad also offers features like Larger Text and Bold Text, which are akin to adjusting the font size of a book to your liking. It's about customizing your reading experience, ensuring that the text on the screen is easy on your eyes, and information is always within comfortable reach.

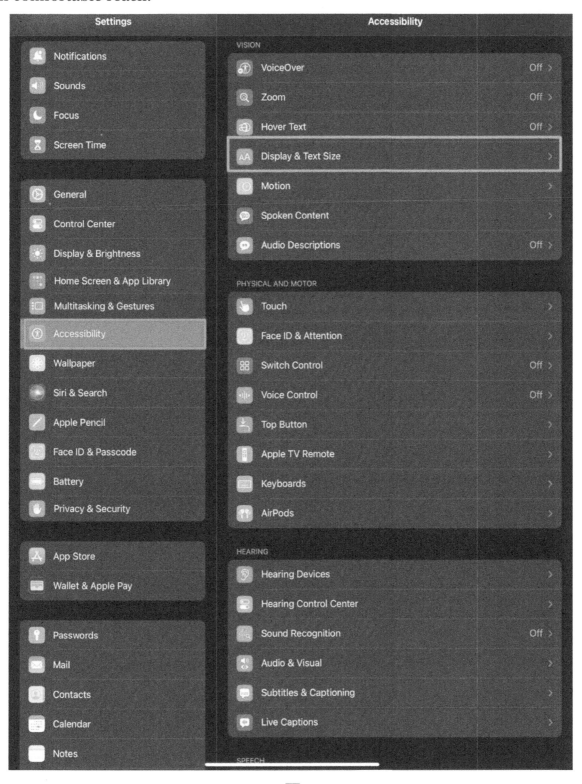

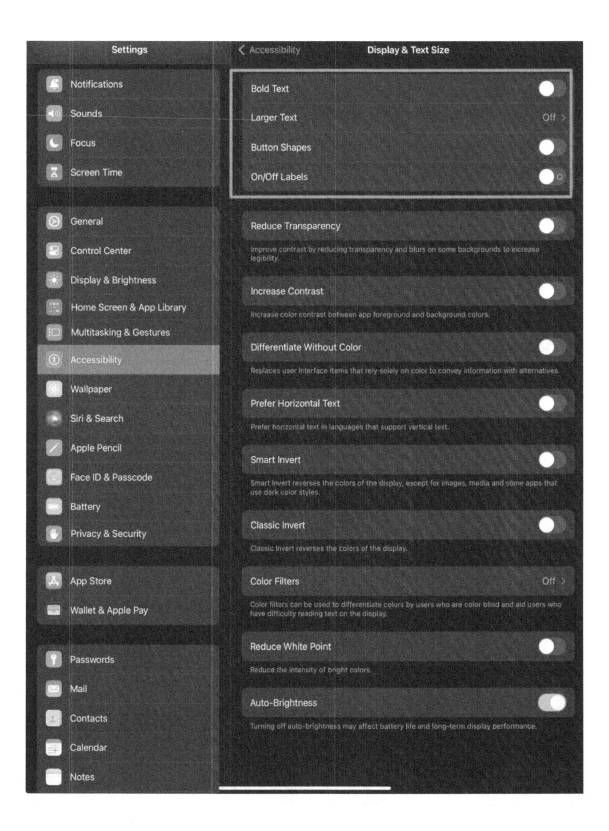

For individuals with hearing impairments, the iPad comes equipped with features like subtitles and Mono Audio. Subtitles ensure that you don't miss a word of dialogue in videos or FaceTime calls, while Mono Audio consolidates sound into a single stream, making it easier to listen to music or podcasts, especially if you have hearing loss in one ear.

But the iPad's inclusivity doesn't stop there. For those who find it challenging to use a touchscreen, AssistiveTouch creates a customizable interface, allowing you to navigate your iPad with simple taps. It's like having a set of digital shortcuts at your fingertips, turning complex gestures into simple ones.

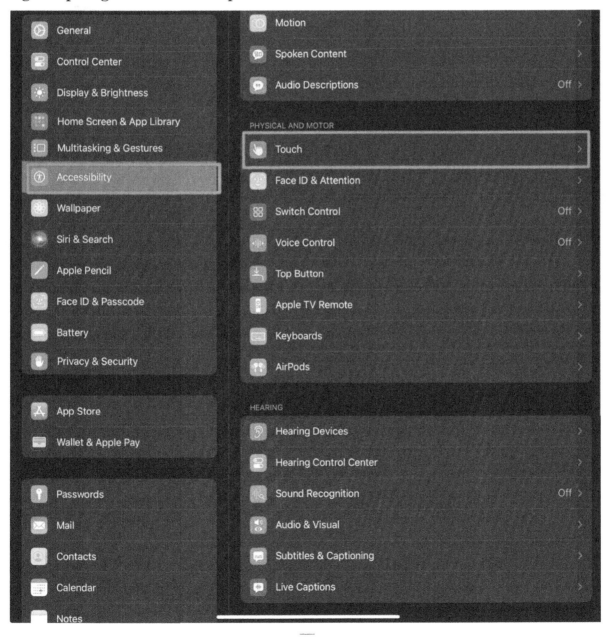

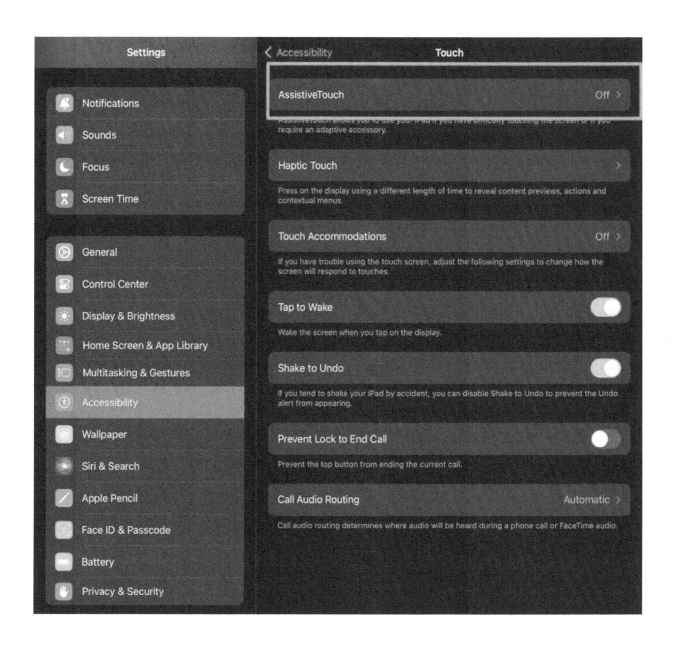

Switch Control is another groundbreaking feature, designed for individuals with limited physical mobility. It allows you to interact with your iPad using adaptive devices like switches, buttons, or even head movements. This feature turns the iPad into a device that can be navigated with minimal physical interaction, ensuring that everyone, regardless of their physical abilities, can enjoy the iPad experience.

In conclusion, the accessibility features of the iPad are more than just technological advancements; they are a testament to Apple's commitment to inclusivity. These features ensure that the iPad is not just a device for the few but a companion for the many. They represent the ethos that technology should bring people together, erase boundaries, and create a world where everyone has equal access to the wonders of the digital age. With these features, the iPad becomes not just a tool for entertainment or communication, but a bridge to a more inclusive, accessible world.

As you conclude setting up your new iPad, you stand at the gateway of a new realm of possibilities. Your device is now a reflection of your personal preferences, equipped with the tools to ensure a secure and inclusive experience. Whether it's the ease of connecting to your world, the security of your personal data, or the accessibility that makes the iPad a device for everyone, your journey has been about making this technology truly yours. The steps you have taken are the foundation of a relationship with a device that promises to bring convenience, connection, and joy into your daily life. Your iPad is now ready to accompany you on your digital adventures, bringing the world closer with every tap and swipe.

Chapter 3. Understanding the iPad Interface

Embarking on the journey of understanding the iPad interface is like stepping into a beautifully designed garden, where each pathway leads to a new discovery. The interface of your iPad, with its intuitive design and user-friendly features, is crafted to enhance your digital experience, making every interaction feel natural and effortless. From the welcoming Home Screen to the indispensable Siri, each element is thoughtfully placed to bring convenience and efficiency to your fingertips. This guide is your companion in exploring the seamless integration of technology and design, helping you navigate the various aspects of the iPad interface with ease and confidence. As you delve into this exploration, you will find that your iPad is more than just a device; it's a portal to a world of possibilities, tailored to your personal needs and preferences.

Home Screen and App Icons

The Home Screen of your iPad is akin to the welcoming front porch of a home, a place where everything you need is neatly arranged and easily accessible. It's the starting point of your digital adventure, a familiar and comforting space where your journey with your iPad begins each day. This screen is not just a collection of icons; it's a carefully curated gallery of your digital life, representing the apps and tools that you hold dear.

As you gaze upon the Home Screen, you'll notice the array of app icons, each a portal to a different experience. These icons are more than just colorful squares on a screen; they are like doorways to different rooms, each with its own purpose and story. From the green pastures of the Photos app, where your memories are stored, to the bustling marketplace of the App Store, where the world's creativity is at your fingertips, each app opens up a new realm for exploration.

Navigating the Home Screen is an intuitive experience, akin to walking through a well-organized garden, where every path leads to a different flowerbed. Swiping between screens, you wander through different sections of your digital garden, discovering new apps and tools. The fluidity of this experience makes the journey through your Home Screen not just easy but enjoyable.

Personalizing your Home Screen is like arranging the furniture in your living room. You can move the app icons around, grouping them by their function or your frequency of use. Some prefer to have their most-used apps, like Messages or Mail, in the dock for easy access, while others might choose to keep a beloved photo editing app or a frequently visited news app front and center. This personalization makes your iPad truly yours, reflecting your preferences and lifestyle.

The iPad's Home Screen also allows for the creation of folders, a feature akin to putting together a personal library. By grouping similar apps into folders, you create a sense of order and accessibility. It's like having a bookshelf where all your novels are sorted by genre, making it easy to find exactly what you're looking for.

The design of the Home Screen is a testament to the iPad's philosophy of balance between functionality and aesthetics. The icons are designed to be recognizable at a glance, with vibrant colors and simple imagery. This clarity is like having a well-labeled map; you always know where you are and where you want to go. The beauty of the Home Screen lies in its simplicity – it doesn't overwhelm but invites exploration.

As you interact with your Home Screen each day, it becomes a reflection of your journey with your iPad. With each app you download, each folder you create, and each rearrangement you make, the Home Screen evolves, mirroring the changes in your digital habits and preferences. It's a dynamic canvas that grows with you, a constant in the ever-changing world of technology.

In essence, the Home Screen and app icons of your iPad are the foundations of your digital experience. They offer a starting point for all your tasks, entertainment, and explorations. This interface is designed not just for functionality but for comfort and personalization, making your interaction with the iPad not just efficient but uniquely personal. As you continue to use your iPad, the Home Screen becomes more than just a display; it becomes a familiar friend, a space that is distinctly and wonderfully yours.

The Dock: Your Essential Apps

The Dock on your iPad is a testament to the art of convenience and efficiency, much like the favorite corner of a craftsman's workshop where the most important tools are within arm's reach. It's a special area at the bottom of your Home Screen, not merely a part of the interface but a dynamic and essential element that enhances your interaction with your iPad. The Dock is where you place the apps that are integral to your daily digital life, making them readily accessible regardless of where you are in the sea of apps and pages.

Think of the Dock as your personal command center. Just as a captain of a ship has the most crucial instruments and controls immediately available, the Dock lets you access your most frequently used apps with a simple tap. This could include your email, your preferred news app, or a digital notebook. It's tailored to fit your unique needs and habits, ensuring that your most treasured tools are always just a touch away.

Customizing the Dock is akin to arranging your favorite books on a shelf or placing your most cherished photographs on a mantelpiece. You can add apps to the Dock by simply dragging them down to this special area. It's a gesture that signifies importance and preference, marking these apps as your chosen few in a world full of options. The process is intuitive and straightforward, reflecting the iPad's commitment to user-centric design.

The beauty of the Dock lies in its fluidity and adaptability. It's not a static row of icons; it's a dynamic space that changes as your day progresses. During a morning routine, it might hold your calendar and news app. By evening, it could transform to display your favorite streaming service and a relaxing game. This flexibility is like having a living space that rearranges itself to suit your mood and activities.

Moreover, the Dock isn't just about quick access; it's about enhancing your multitasking capabilities. With the Dock, switching between apps becomes a seamless dance, a graceful movement from one task to another. It's an essential tool for those who juggle various activities – from checking emails to editing a photo or jotting down notes. This fluidity transforms the way you interact with your iPad, making multitasking not just possible but enjoyable.

The Dock also subtly encourages exploration and experimentation. It invites you to consider which apps are truly essential to your daily life and perhaps to discover new ones that could take their place in this honored row. It's a space that evolves with your preferences, adapting to your changing needs and interests.

So, the Dock on your iPad is a reflection of your lifestyle, habits, and preferences. It represents the core of your iPad usage, a space where convenience meets personalization. As you use your iPad, the Dock becomes more than just a feature; it becomes a companion in your digital journey, a constant that provides both comfort and efficiency. It's a simple yet powerful aspect of the iPad interface that enhances your experience, ensuring that the tools you need are always at your fingertips, ready to assist, entertain, and enrich your digital life.

Control Center: Quick Access to Tools

The Control Center on your iPad is akin to a magician's hat, filled with an array of tools and tricks that are both practical and enchanting. This feature is more than just a menu; it's a customizable command panel that provides instant access to the tools and settings you use most frequently. Imagine having a sleek, digital Swiss Army knife at your fingertips, ready to deploy whatever tool you need with just a swipe and a tap.

Accessing the Control Center is a gesture as simple and natural as flicking a light switch. With a swipe down from the top-right corner of your screen, this panel gracefully slides into view, revealing a constellation of icons that represent various functionalities. Each icon in the Control Center is a shortcut to an action or a setting, allowing you to adjust your iPad to your immediate needs without delving into the depths of settings menus.

One of the most striking features of the Control Center is its adaptability and customization. You have the power to choose which controls appear in this panel, tailoring it to fit your unique lifestyle and usage patterns. It's like arranging your toolshed or kitchen drawers, where you keep your most essential tools within easy reach. From the flashlight to the calculator, from screen brightness to volume control, each element of the Control Center can be handpicked to ensure that your most-needed tools are always just a swipe away.

Moreover, the Control Center is a hub of convenience for managing your multimedia experience. It allows you to control music playback, adjust volume levels, and connect to audio devices effortlessly. Imagine sitting in your favorite chair, using the Control Center to orchestrate the soundtrack of your evening, all without interrupting the flow of your activities.

The brilliance of the Control Center extends to its role in managing connectivity. With quick toggles for Wi-Fi, Bluetooth, and Airplane Mode, it acts as a command bridge for how your iPad interacts with the world. Whether you're stepping into a flight and need to switch to Airplane Mode, or you're starting your day by reconnecting to Wi-Fi, these actions are simplified into a single tap, encapsulating the essence of efficiency and ease.

Another aspect of the Control Center is its contribution to the personalization of your iPad experience. It includes controls for features like Do Not Disturb and screen mirroring, empowering you to dictate how and when you want to focus or share your content. It's like having a personal assistant who understands your preferences and adjusts the environment accordingly.

So, the Control Center on your iPad is more than just a set of quick access tools; it's a testament to the device's focus on user-centric design. It provides a level of convenience and customization that transforms your interaction with your iPad, making it more intuitive, more efficient, and more enjoyable. The Control Center is not just a feature; it's a companion that enhances your digital journey, ensuring that the tools you need are always at your service, ready to assist, facilitate, and enrich your experience with your iPad.

Notifications and Alerts

Navigating through the digital landscape of your iPad, notifications and alerts act as signposts and messengers, keeping you informed and connected. These small, yet significant signals are not mere interruptions; they are the threads that connect you to the tapestry of your digital life. They are the gentle taps on the shoulder, the soft chimes in the background, reminding you of meetings, messages, and moments that matter.

Notifications on your iPad come in various forms, each serving a unique purpose. They are like the diverse calls of a bustling marketplace, each vendor vying for your attention, offering news, reminders, and updates. Some notifications are brief pop-ups, like a whisper in your ear, giving you a quick glimpse of an email or a message. Others appear as banners at the top of your screen, a more persistent reminder that lingers just long enough for you to take notice.

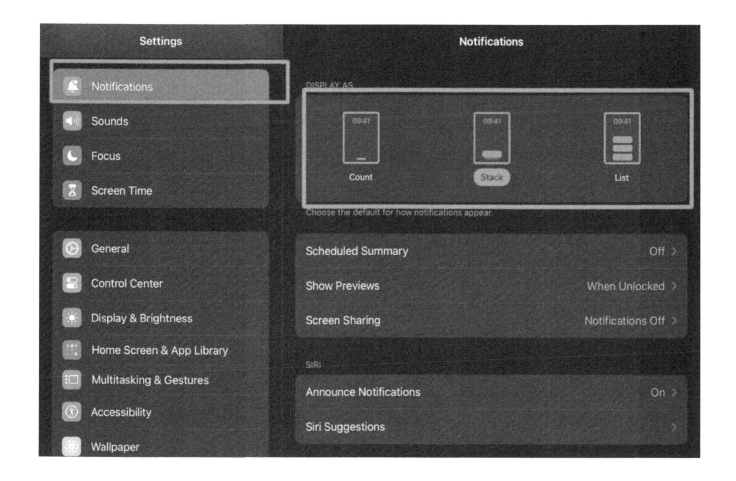

Managing these notifications is akin to conducting an orchestra; each alert has its place and time, contributing to the harmony of your day. The iPad empowers you to fine-tune this symphony. With a few taps in the Settings, you can choose which apps send you notifications, how they present themselves, and when they appear. It's like setting the rules for your personal concert, ensuring that each alert harmonizes with your life's rhythm, neither overwhelming nor going unnoticed.

The subtle art of balancing these alerts lies in prioritizing what matters most. Do you need to be reminded of every email as it arrives, or would a summary suffice? Is a breaking news alert a must, or can it wait until you have a quiet moment? These decisions shape the nature of your interaction with your iPad, tailoring the notification experience to suit your lifestyle, your work, and your preferences.

But it's not just about managing distractions; it's about staying connected to what matters. Alerts for calendar events act as gentle nudges, ensuring you never miss an important meeting or a family gathering. Message notifications keep the lines of communication open, bridging distances with a tap. Each alert, each notification, serves as a connection point to the people, projects, and passions that populate your world.

Notifications also extend to the realm of app updates and system alerts. They are like the subtle cues from a co-pilot, keeping you informed about the latest features, security updates, and improvements. These alerts ensure that your iPad experience is always at its peak, providing you with the latest tools and safeguards.

In conclusion, notifications and alerts on your iPad are the subtle yet significant elements that enhance your digital journey. They are the whispers and cues that keep you in sync with your online world. Like a skilled navigator reading signs and signals, managing these notifications allows you to sail smoothly through your day, staying informed, connected, and in control. In the hands of a mindful user, these alerts become more than just digital noise; they transform into a curated stream of information, each serving a purpose, each adding value to the rich experience of using your iPad.

Using Siri for Voice Commands

In the world of the iPad, Siri stands as a remarkable testament to the fusion of technology and human-like interaction, a virtual assistant that brings a touch of magic to your daily digital experience. Siri is more than a voice recognition system; it's a conversational companion, ready to assist with a wide array of tasks, making your interactions with the iPad feel more natural, more intuitive, and strikingly human.

Imagine having a personal assistant who is always just a voice command away, eager to help with everything from setting reminders to finding information online. Siri is that assistant, living within your iPad, always ready to respond to your queries and commands. It's like having a knowledgeable friend who's always available to offer assistance, advice, and even a bit of humor.

Engaging with Siri is as simple as having a conversation. You activate Siri with a press of a button or a simple "Hey Siri," and then the digital magic unfolds. Siri's interface is designed to be as natural as speaking to another person. You ask a question or make a request, and Siri responds with the relevant information or action. It's a seamless interaction that blurs the line between technology and human communication.

The capabilities of Siri are vast and varied, much like the skill set of a talented multitasker. Need to send a quick message? Just tell Siri what you want to say and to whom. Looking for directions to a new restaurant? Ask Siri, and you'll have your route in seconds. Want to know the weather forecast? Siri can tell you whether to grab an umbrella before you head out. Each task, no matter how big or small, is handled with efficiency and a touch of personality.

But Siri's talents go beyond performing tasks; it's also about enhancing your iPad experience. Siri can suggest apps you might like, find documents you need, and even identify songs playing in the background. It's like having a personal concierge who not only knows your preferences but also anticipates your needs.

Moreover, Siri is adaptable and learns from your interactions. Over time, it becomes more attuned to your voice, your manner of speaking, and your preferences. This learning process is not just about improving accuracy; it's about creating a more personalized experience. Siri evolves to become more in sync with your digital habits and lifestyle, much like a close friend who gets to know you better over time.

Privacy and security are also integral to Siri's design. Your interactions with Siri are protected, ensuring that your personal information and queries remain confidential. It's a system built on trust, respecting your privacy while providing a personalized experience.

In conclusion, Siri is a defining feature of your iPad, a symbol of modern technological wonders. It brings a level of interaction that is profoundly human and incredibly efficient. Using Siri for voice commands is not just about convenience; it's about experiencing a new way of interacting with technology, where your voice becomes the bridge between your needs and your iPad's vast capabilities. Siri is more than a feature; it's a companion, a helper, and a significant step towards a future where technology understands and responds to us in the most natural way possible.

As you continue to use and explore your iPad, you carry with you the knowledge that this device is more than just a tool; it's a companion that adapts, responds, and grows with you.

Chapter 4. Navigating with Touch and Gestures

Embarking on the exploration of touch and gestures with your iPad is to enter a world where technology and intuition dance in perfect harmony. This chapter delves into the subtle art of navigating your device using gestures that are as natural and fluid as the movements of your own hands. From the foundational simplicity of tapping and swiping to the more intricate ballet of multi-touch commands and zooming, each gesture is a key that unlocks new dimensions of interaction with your iPad. As you learn these gestures, you'll discover that they are not just methods of control but extensions of your own intentions, enabling a seamless and enjoyable experience that enhances every interaction with your digital companion.

Basic Touch Gestures Explained

Embarking on the journey of navigating your iPad, the exploration of basic touch gestures is akin to learning the essential notes of a new musical instrument. Each gesture - a tap, a swipe, a scroll - harmonizes to create a symphony of interaction between you and your device, a language spoken not with words but with the fluid dance of your fingers on the screen.

The tap is the most fundamental of these gestures, as instinctive as a nod in conversation. It's the way you select items, open apps, and interact with various elements on your screen. This gesture is akin to pointing at an object of interest; a gentle press on the screen and the iPad responds, opening doors into apps and menus with graceful ease.

Swiping on your iPad is like turning the pages of a cherished book. It's the gesture that navigates you through content on your screen. This fluid motion, a graceful arc drawn by your finger, allows you to traverse your digital landscape with ease. Whether flipping through photos, scrolling through a webpage, or transitioning between pages on the Home Screen, swiping is your intuitive guide.

The scroll, a continuous vertical swipe, brings the experience of strolling through a serene garden into the digital realm. It moves you up and down within apps and pages, revealing content as you go. This gesture immerses you in your digital environment, whether you're engrossed in a captivating article, browsing a list, or exploring a lengthy document.

For quicker navigation, the flick comes into play. Think of it as the brisk, efficient cousin of the swipe, a gesture that propels content rapidly across the screen. It's a swift movement, reminiscent of skimming stones across water, ideal for swiftly traversing long distances within your iPad.

Understanding and incorporating these touch gestures transforms your interaction with the iPad. Each movement, from the deliberate tap to the swift flick, becomes a note in your digital symphony. The tap is your precise point of contact, the swipe and scroll your pathways of exploration, and the flick your quick leap across the digital terrain.

Mastering these gestures marks the beginning of a deeper connection with your iPad. It elevates your experience from simple usage to a form of expressive interaction. These gestures form the foundational language of your device, a dialect that is universally intuitive yet uniquely personal. As you continue to engage with your iPad, these gestures will become an extension of your digital intent, enabling a seamless and intuitive journey through your technological world.

Scrolling, Swiping, and Tapping

In the landscape of the iPad's interface, the actions of scrolling, swiping, and tapping form the core of your navigational experience. These gestures are the conduit through which you engage with your digital environment, as natural and intuitive as the movements in a well-choreographed dance. Each of these gestures, simple in its execution yet profound in its functionality, transforms the way you interact with your iPad, turning every action into a seamless and harmonious experience.

Let's start with scrolling, a gesture as fundamental as walking in the physical world. Scrolling is your tool for traversing vertically or horizontally across content. It's the motion you use to journey through lengthy articles, explore extensive lists, or move through your photo library. This gesture mimics the natural action of moving a piece of paper up and down or side to side. It's a continuous, fluid motion, like gliding your fingers over the surface of a tranquil lake, causing ripples that extend across the digital canvas of your screen.

Swiping, on the other hand, is the gesture of transition and exploration. It's the movement you use to navigate between different pages on your Home Screen, to dismiss notifications, or to open the Control Center. Swiping is a broader, more defining gesture compared to scrolling. It's akin to turning a page in a book or drawing back a curtain to reveal a new scene. The swipe is an expression of intent, a clear command to your iPad to move you from one environment to another, from one state of engagement to the next.

Tapping is perhaps the most precise and targeted of gestures. It is the equivalent of pointing to something specific, a way of selecting, of making choices. When you tap an app icon, you're giving a clear instruction to open it. When you tap a link, you're deciding to explore further. Tapping is the digital equivalent of pressing a button; it's a deliberate and focused action, a fundamental tool for interaction within the digital realm of your iPad.

The beauty of these gestures lies in their inherent intuitiveness and simplicity. They are not just methods of navigation but are extensions of your natural movements. There's a rhythm to scrolling, swiping, and tapping that resonates with the innate human understanding of movement and space. These gestures are as much a part of the iPad experience as the apps and content they navigate.

Furthermore, the consistency of these gestures across various apps and contexts on the iPad ensures a smooth, unified user experience. Whether you're reading an ebook, browsing the internet, or checking your emails, the way you scroll, swipe, and tap remains constant, a universal language that you speak across all your digital interactions.

These gestures also represent the convergence of technology and human ergonomics. Designed with the user in mind, they make the interaction with the iPad feel natural, reducing the learning curve and making technology accessible to all ages and abilities. They encapsulate the philosophy that technology should adapt to the user, not the other way around.

In essence, scrolling, swiping, and tapping on your iPad are not just touch gestures; they are the foundational elements of your interaction with the device. They bring fluidity, control, and ease to your digital navigation, transforming your engagement with the iPad from mere usage to an intuitive, enjoyable experience. As you continue to explore and utilize these gestures, they become second nature, an integral part of your digital language, enhancing your journey through the ever-expanding world of technology.

Mastering Drag and Drop

In the realm of touch and gestures on your iPad, mastering the art of drag and drop is akin to learning a graceful dance, a movement that adds a layer of sophistication and fluidity to your digital interactions. This feature, an elegant testament to the iPad's advanced capabilities, transforms the way you organize and manage content, merging simplicity with powerful functionality. It's a ballet of fingers on the screen, where objects respond to your touch with a harmonious blend of precision and ease.

Imagine holding a photograph in your hands. You decide where to place it on a wall, moving it around until it fits perfectly into its new location. Drag and drop on the iPad offers a similar experience. Whether it's a document, an image, or even a link, you can move it seamlessly from one place to another. This gesture is more than just shifting content; it's about reimagining how you organize and interact with your digital environment.

The process begins with a simple touch, a press and hold on the item you wish to move. It's a moment of connection, where the digital object adheres to your fingertip as if by magic. As you move your finger across the screen, the item follows, floating over the interface like a leaf carried by a gentle stream. This motion is intuitive, a natural extension of your intention, guided by the tactile feedback of the screen.

But drag and drop is not just a solitary act; it's a dance that can involve multiple partners. You can gather several items together, bundling them with a few taps, and then move them as a group. This capability transforms tasks that were once tedious into a symphony of efficiency. Organizing your photos, rearranging apps, or compiling documents becomes a task of ease and enjoyment.

The true elegance of drag and drop lies in its versatility across different apps and contexts. You can drag a photo from your gallery into an email, drop a link into a message, or even rearrange files in your file management app. Each action feels seamless and integrated, as if the iPad is anticipating your needs, adapting to your workflow.

Moreover, the drag and drop feature exemplifies the iPad's commitment to user-centric design. It acknowledges that the digital world is not just about consumption but also about creation and organization. By enabling you to manipulate digital objects with such ease, the iPad empowers you to take control of your digital space, turning it into an extension of your personal and professional life.

Mastering drag and drop on your iPad opens up a new dimension of interaction. It's a feature that brings a tactile, almost physical quality to your digital experience. The satisfaction of dropping an item into its new place is tangible, a small triumph in your everyday tasks.

In essence, drag and drop is more than a gesture; it's a tool that epitomizes the iPad's philosophy of intuitive interaction. It elevates the touch experience from mere navigation to tactile management of your digital universe. As you become adept at this dance of drag and drop, you'll find that your iPad is not just a device you use; it's a space you curate, an environment that you shape and refine with the tips of your fingers.

Multi-Touch Gestures

Delving into the realm of multi-touch gestures on the iPad is like discovering a hidden language of digital expression, where the use of multiple fingers simultaneously unlocks a new dimension of interaction. These gestures are a ballet of touch, a chorus of fingers working in harmony to command the digital stage of your iPad. This orchestration of touch is not just an advanced feature; it's a symphony of usability and functionality, enhancing the way you engage with your device.

Multi-touch gestures on the iPad go beyond the basic tap and swipe, inviting you to use two, three, or even four fingers to perform actions that are both complex and intuitive. These gestures are like chords in music, where the combination of notes creates a harmony richer than any single note could achieve. They transform the iPad from a solo instrument into an ensemble, capable of more nuanced and sophisticated performances.

One of the most fundamental multi-touch gestures is the pinch. This gesture, performed by bringing two fingers together or moving them apart on the screen, is akin to zooming in and out with a camera lens. It's a motion as natural as focusing your eyes on an object near or far. The pinch gesture allows you to dive into the details of a photo, expand the view of a map, or adjust the size of text and images, bringing the digital world closer or giving you a wider perspective.

Then there's the rotation gesture, where you place two fingers on the screen and twist them around each other. This gesture is like turning a key in a lock or adjusting a dial. It's used to rotate images, maps, or other elements on your screen, giving you control over their orientation. The rotation gesture is a dance of precision and control, allowing you to align your digital environment to your exact specifications.

Another multi-touch marvel is the swipe with multiple fingers. A three-finger swipe can be used to navigate through apps or close them. It's like sweeping a path through leaves with a brush; with each stroke, you clear the way, moving effortlessly between tasks. This gesture enhances multitasking, allowing you to switch between applications with a fluidity that feels almost magical.

The four-finger swipe upwards reveals the app switcher, a gesture that feels like opening a treasure chest, unveiling all your open applications. This gesture is about having an overview, a bird's eye view of your digital landscape, enabling you to navigate with a sense of mastery and overview.

These multi-touch gestures, while sophisticated, are rooted in intuitive movements. They echo the natural actions of the human hand, from the pinch of a thumb and forefinger to the sweep of the palm. They are a testament to the iPad's design philosophy, which seeks to bridge the gap between technology and human instinct.

Engaging with these multi-touch gestures deepens your relationship with your iPad. They turn everyday interactions into a dance of fingers on glass, a dance that is both functional and beautiful. As you become more proficient in this multi-touch language, your iPad becomes an extension of your own gestures, responding to the nuances of your touch with precision and grace.

These gestures are not just tools; they are an expression of the potential of human-technology interaction. They represent the harmony that can be achieved when digital devices respond to the most natural and instinctive human movements. As you master these multi-touch gestures, you unlock the full potential of your iPad, turning every interaction into an opportunity for creativity, efficiency, and elegance.

Zooming In and Out for Better Visibility

The art of zooming in and out on your iPad is akin to adjusting a telescope, bringing the stars of the digital universe into focus. This gesture is not just about magnifying what's on your screen; it's about enhancing your visibility, ensuring that every detail, text, or image is clear and accessible. In the realm of touch and gestures, zooming in and out is a testament to the iPad's commitment to adaptability and personalized user experience.

Imagine standing before a grand canvas, a painting rich in detail and color. Zooming in is like stepping closer, allowing you to appreciate the intricacies and subtleties of the artwork. On your iPad, this gesture lets you delve into the finer points of a photo, examine the nuances of a map, or enlarge the text to a comfortable reading size. It's a gesture that brings the world within your screen into sharp relief, making the digital landscape more intimate and comprehensible.

Zooming out, in contrast, is like stepping back to take in the whole picture. It provides a broader view, a wider perspective that helps you orient yourself within the digital environment. On your iPad, this gesture is crucial for getting an overview of a webpage, seeing an entire document at once, or gaining a comprehensive view of a large image. Zooming out is about understanding context, seeing how the details fit into the larger scheme.

This zooming gesture is performed with a simple pinch or spread of your fingers. It's a motion as instinctive as gesturing with your hands while speaking, as natural as reaching out to touch something of interest. When you pinch your fingers together on the screen, the content shrinks away, giving you a broader view. When you spread your fingers apart, the content expands, bringing details into focus. This motion is fluid, responsive, and precise, mirroring the natural movements of your hands.

The beauty of this gesture lies in its simplicity and universality. It doesn't require memorizing complex commands or navigating through menus. It's as straightforward as touching the screen, a direct and intuitive way to adjust what you see. This simplicity belies the powerful technology at work, technology that responds to the most natural human impulses.

Zooming in and out also plays a vital role in accessibility. For those with visual impairments, this gesture is a key tool for making the digital world accessible. It breaks down barriers, ensuring that everyone can enjoy the richness and variety of content on their iPad. This gesture exemplifies the inclusive design of the iPad, a design that acknowledges and accommodates a diverse range of users.

In essence, the ability to zoom in and out on your iPad is more than a feature; it's a gateway to clarity and understanding. It empowers you to explore the digital landscape on your terms, to adjust your view according to your needs and curiosity. As you use this gesture, you'll find that it enriches your interaction with your iPad, bringing the world within your screen to life in vivid detail. It's a testament to the power of touch and technology working in harmony, enhancing your digital experience in the most natural and intuitive way.

This newfound fluency in the language of touch empowers you to navigate your iPad with confidence and grace, making every interaction a seamless extension of your digital life.

Chapter 5. Personalizing Your iPad

Embarking on the personalization of your iPad is a journey akin to tailoring a fine garment to fit your unique style and preferences. This exploration is dedicated to transforming your iPad from a standard technological device into a reflection of your individuality and way of life. The art of customization extends from the aesthetic delight of selecting wallpapers and themes to the practical organization of apps and settings. Each step in this process is not just about alteration, but about creating an experience that harmonically resonates with your personal rhythm. Discovering these customization options unveils the joy and empowerment of crafting a device that truly feels personal, making every interaction with your iPad a reflection of your unique self.

Changing Wallpaper and Themes

Personalizing your iPad begins with the transformation of its visual interface, a process akin to setting the stage for a personal theater where technology meets individuality. Changing the wallpaper and themes on your iPad is not just about altering a background image; it's an expression of your personality, a reflection of your style, and a statement of your preferences. This customization transforms your iPad from a standard device into a personal artifact, resonating with your unique essence.

Imagine your iPad as a canvas, and the wallpaper as the painting that defines its aesthetic. The choice of wallpaper can set the mood, evoke emotions, or remind you of cherished memories. Whether it's a photo of a stunning landscape, a piece of abstract art, or a snapshot of a loved one, each image adds a layer of personalization to your iPad experience. This visual element is the first thing you see when you unlock your device, making it integral to how you perceive and interact with your iPad.

The process of changing the wallpaper is as simple as it is impactful. You delve into the settings, where a gallery of images awaits your selection – each one a potential backdrop for your digital adventures. Apple provides a variety of built-in options, from dynamic images that shift with your device's movement to stills that capture the tranquility of nature or the vibrancy of abstract patterns. These choices are curated to cater to a wide range of tastes and preferences, ensuring that every user finds something that resonates with their personal style.

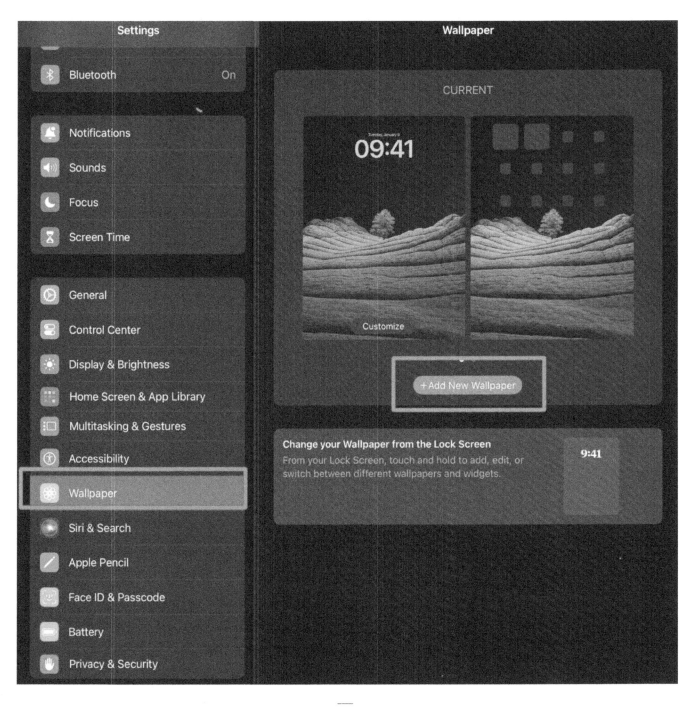

But the customization doesn't stop with Apple's offerings. The true beauty of this feature lies in the ability to use your own photos. This option transforms the wallpaper into a deeply personal statement. A family photo turns your iPad into a digital frame, keeping your loved ones close. A picture from your travels makes your device a window to past adventures. Each personal photo you choose as your wallpaper is a celebration of a moment, a story captured in time, lending an intimate touch to your digital space.

Themes, though more subtle than wallpapers, play a significant role in personalizing your iPad. They influence the overall look of your interface, from the color of your folders to the appearance of your dock. Adjusting these elements allows you to tailor the visual experience of your device to suit your mood and needs. It's like choosing the perfect outfit for your digital companion, one that complements its functionality with aesthetic harmony.

Personalizing your iPad with different wallpapers and themes is more than a cosmetic change; it's about making your device truly yours. It's a reflection of your personality, your tastes, and your experiences. This customization makes each interaction with your iPad more enjoyable and meaningful. It turns a standard device into a personal diary, a gallery of memories, a reflection of your individual journey.

In essence, the act of personalizing your iPad through changing wallpapers and themes is a celebration of individuality in the digital age. It's an opportunity to imprint your personality onto your device, making every use a more personal and intimate experience. This level of customization not only enhances the aesthetic appeal of your iPad but also strengthens your emotional connection to it, making it an extension of your personal world.

Organizing Apps into Folders

Organizing apps into folders on your iPad is akin to curating a personal library, where every book is thoughtfully placed for easy access and aesthetic harmony. This process of organization is not merely about tidiness; it's a reflection of your lifestyle, your priorities, and how you interact with your digital environment. By creating folders, you transform your iPad from a mere collection of apps into a well-arranged ensemble that resonates with your personal rhythm.

Picture yourself walking through a garden where every plant is meticulously placed, each path leading you to a different array of flowers. In the digital garden of your iPad, each folder is a path, leading you to a group of apps that serve a specific purpose in your life. These folders are the result of your careful planning and organization, a testament to your understanding of how you use, prioritize, and value your apps.

The process of creating a folder is as intuitive as it is meaningful. It begins with a simple drag and drop – a gesture that feels natural yet purposeful. You select an app and gently move it onto another app that shares a similar function or category. This simple movement is like tying two threads together, creating a bond between the apps. The iPad responds to this gesture by creating a new folder, a new space that holds these apps together, under a name that you choose – a name that signifies the purpose or the theme of this newly formed group.

As you continue this process, you start crafting a landscape on your Home Screen that mirrors your preferences and needs. You might create a folder for your favorite games, a sanctuary for leisure and entertainment. Another folder might house your productivity apps, a toolbox for your work and creative endeavors. Each folder you create is a reflection of an aspect of your life, neatly categorized and easily accessible.

This organization goes beyond mere convenience; it's about creating a space that feels familiar and comfortable. When you open your iPad, you are greeted with a view that makes sense to you, where every app has its place, and you know exactly where to find what you need. It's a sense of order that brings calm to the potential chaos of a digital world brimming with applications and services.

Customizing these folders with names and arranging them on your Home Screen adds another layer of personalization. The way you name and position these folders is a representation of how you think and operate. A folder named 'Travel' might sit on your first page, a constant reminder of your passion for exploration, while a folder named 'Daily Tools' could be positioned for quick access, ready to assist you in your everyday tasks.

In essence, organizing your apps into folders is a choreography of your digital life. It's a practice that not only declutters your virtual space but also aligns it with your personal habits and preferences. This organization enhances your interaction with the iPad, making every use more efficient and enjoyable. As you tailor your Home Screen with folders, your iPad becomes more than a device; it transforms into a personalized companion, a reflection of your world organized into the palm of your hand.

Customizing the Dock

Customizing the Dock on your iPad is akin to arranging the most cherished tools in a craftsman's workshop, ensuring that everything you need for your digital journey is within easy reach. This act of personalization is more than a mere adjustment of settings; it's about tailoring your device to fit the unique contours of your digital lifestyle. The Dock, with its capacity to house your most-used apps, becomes a reflection of your priorities, habits, and preferences, thus transforming it into a personalized command center that resonates with your individual rhythm and routine.

Envision the Dock as a shelf in your personal study, where you keep your favorite books and mementos. Each app you place in the Dock is like a book that you often refer to, a tool you frequently need, or a keepsake that brings joy. The process of selecting these apps is thoughtful and deliberate. You might choose the email app that connects you to friends and colleagues, the calendar app that keeps your life organized, or the music app that provides the soundtrack to your days. These choices are not random; they are deeply personal, shaping the way you interact with your iPad on a fundamental level.

Customizing the Dock is a straightforward yet impactful process. With a simple touch and drag, you can add apps to the Dock or remove those you use less frequently. This gesture, much like rearranging items on a desk for optimal comfort and efficiency, allows you to design a Dock that truly aligns with how you use your iPad. The ease of this customization process is a testament to the iPad's user-centric design, which empowers you to make your device truly your own.

Moreover, the Dock's dynamic nature adds to its utility. It adapts to your recent applications, subtly changing to reflect your current activities. This feature is like having a smart assistant who remembers your recent tasks and keeps your tools ready for you. Whether you're working on a document, browsing the web, or editing photos, the Dock evolves with you, providing a seamless transition between tasks.

The customization of the Dock also extends to how it behaves in different contexts. You can decide whether it appears on the Home Screen, stays hidden while using apps, or reveals itself with a simple swipe. This level of control allows you to dictate how you interact with your iPad, whether you prefer a constant view of your essential apps or a cleaner interface that maximizes screen space.

In essence, customizing the Dock on your iPad is about creating a space that is intuitively yours. It's about arranging your digital environment in a way that enhances your productivity, suits your habits, and brings joy to your daily interactions. The Dock becomes more than just a feature; it's a personalized aspect of your iPad experience, a testament to the device's adaptability and alignment with your unique digital life. As you continue to use and customize your iPad, the Dock remains a constant yet adaptable element, a cornerstone of your personalized digital experience.

Adjusting Sound and Display Settings

In the symphony of personalizing your iPad, adjusting the sound and display settings is akin to fine-tuning a musical instrument, ensuring every note and tone resonates perfectly with your preferences. This customization extends beyond mere functionality; it's about shaping the sensory experience of your device to harmonize with your environment and lifestyle. These adjustments allow your iPad to speak to you in a language of light and sound that's uniquely tailored to your needs, enhancing both the functionality and pleasure of your interactions.

The journey of customizing sound settings on your iPad is like composing a melody that plays in tune with your life's rhythm. Whether you prefer the gentle chime of a notification or the vibrant ring of an incoming call, each sound can be adjusted to match your desired level of engagement with your device. The volume controls, the choice of ringtones, and the subtle nuances of alert tones - all these elements can be fine-tuned, creating a soundscape that is both pleasing and functional. It's about ensuring that your iPad communicates with you in a manner that is not disruptive but rather enhancing your day-to-day activities.

Moreover, the customization of sound settings extends to the auditory experience within apps and media. You can adjust the balance and EQ settings for music and videos, tailoring the audio output to suit your preferences or the acoustics of your surroundings. This level of control transforms your iPad into a personal theater or a concert hall, delivering an auditory experience that is rich, clear, and immersive.

On the other side of this sensory customization is the adjustment of display settings, a process that is as vital as setting the correct lighting for a masterpiece painting. The iPad's display settings offer a spectrum of adjustments, from brightness to color temperature, all designed to ensure that your visual experience is comfortable, clear, and enjoyable. Adjusting the brightness not only helps in reducing eye strain but also aids in conserving battery life, making it a balance between comfort and efficiency.

The Night Shift feature, which adjusts the color temperature of your display to the warmer end of the spectrum during the evening, exemplifies the thoughtful design of the iPad. It's like having a device that understands the rhythm of the day, transitioning its display to reduce blue light exposure as night falls, thus promoting better sleep and comfort.

Furthermore, the True Tone technology available on some iPad models takes this personalization a step further. It dynamically adjusts the white balance of the display based on the ambient light in your surroundings. This feature is like having a canvas that subtly shifts its hues to remain consistent and natural under different lighting conditions, ensuring that what you see on the screen is as true to life as possible.

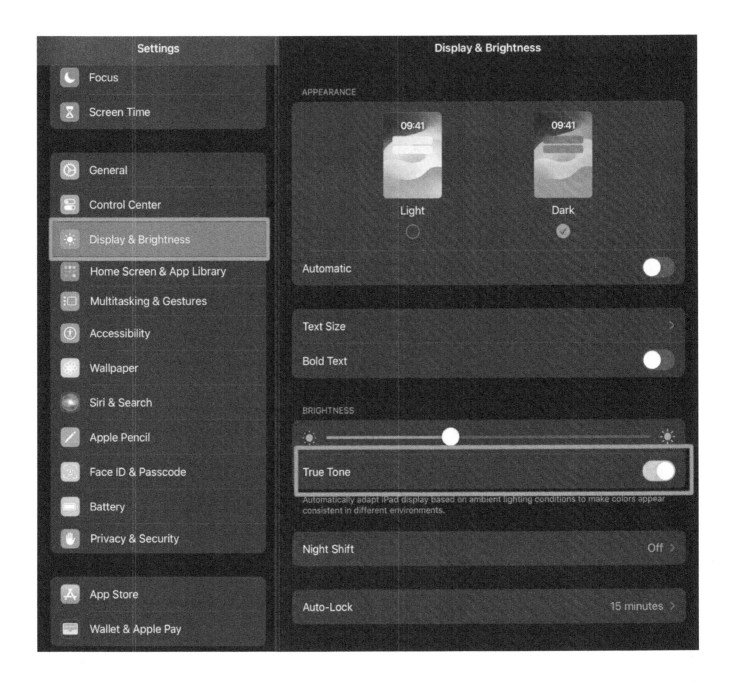

In essence, personalizing the sound and display settings of your iPad is about creating a sensory experience that is in perfect alignment with your personal preferences and needs. It's about making your device feel like an extension of your environment – one that speaks in your preferred tone and illuminates your digital world in the most comfortable and pleasing way. As you continue to explore and adjust these settings, your iPad becomes more than just a tool; it becomes a personalized companion, attuned to your sensory preferences and enhancing your daily digital interactions.

Creating a Customized Experience

Crafting a customized experience on your iPad is like painting a self-portrait; it's a creative process that involves imbuing your device with personal touches that reflect your individuality and preferences. This level of customization is not merely about aesthetics or organization; it's about tailoring your iPad to become an extension of your personality, a digital companion that aligns with your lifestyle, habits, and preferences. It's a journey of transforming a standard device into a unique, personalized tool that resonates with your personal narrative.

This journey of personalization is comprehensive, encompassing every aspect of how you interact with your iPad. It begins with the visual elements, like changing wallpapers and themes, and extends to the organization of apps and adjustment of sound and display settings. But personalization goes beyond these tangible aspects; it delves into configuring settings and features that align with your daily routine, your work style, and even your leisure activities.

Consider the way you arrange your apps and widgets. Like curating exhibits in a museum, you place each app and widget in a way that tells your story. You might prioritize productivity apps, keeping them front and center for easy access during work hours, or you might highlight entertainment and relaxation apps, creating a digital sanctuary for your downtime. This thoughtful arrangement ensures that your iPad reflects and supports your daily routines and preferences.

Customization also involves tailoring notifications and alerts. This process is akin to setting boundaries in your digital life, deciding which apps have the privilege of interrupting you and when. It's about striking a balance between staying connected and maintaining focus. By customizing these alerts, you ensure that your iPad respects your time and attention, becoming a tool that aids your productivity rather than hinders it.

Moreover, personalizing your iPad extends to setting up shortcuts and automations. These powerful tools are like creating a set of personal commandments for your device, instructions that it follows to save you time and effort. Whether it's automating daily tasks or creating shortcuts for complex actions, these configurations make your interactions with your iPad more efficient and aligned with your unique needs.

Accessibility features play a crucial role in personalization too. They allow you to adjust the way you interact with your iPad based on your physical needs and preferences. From adjusting text sizes and contrasts to setting up voice control or custom touch gestures, these features ensure that your iPad is not just a device, but a companion that is attuned to your unique way of navigating the digital world.

In the realm of personalization, even the small details matter. It's about choosing the sounds that your iPad makes, the feedback it provides, and even the way it connects with other devices. Each of these elements contributes to creating an iPad experience that feels like it was crafted just for you.

In essence, creating a customized experience on your iPad is about infusing your device with your essence. It's a process of transformation where technology meets personality, resulting in an iPad that not only serves your needs but also reflects your identity. As you continue to explore and adjust these personalized settings, your iPad becomes more than a tool; it becomes a reflection of you, a canvas where your digital life is painted in your own colors, patterns, and textures. Your iPad, now finely attuned to your preferences, stands ready as a harmonious companion in your digital world.

Chapter 6. Internet and Email

Embarking on the exploration of Internet and Email on your iPad is like setting sail on a digital sea, where currents of information and waves of communication beckon. This realm, abundant with possibilities, demands navigation tools and skills to harness its full potential. Here, you will delve into the art of using Safari, mastering the intricacies of web searches, and establishing a seamless email experience. The journey encompasses setting up your email, understanding the nuances of sending and receiving messages, and curating a collection of bookmarks and favorites. It's about transforming your iPad into a compass and map for this vast digital ocean, ensuring a journey that's not only efficient but also richly rewarding.

Setting Up and Using Safari

Embarking on the journey of setting up and using Safari on your iPad is like opening the door to a vast, vibrant library, where the sum of human knowledge and entertainment is at your fingertips. Safari, Apple's native web browser, is more than just a tool for accessing the internet; it is a gateway to the world, designed with both simplicity and power to enhance your browsing experience. This process of setting up and utilizing Safari is your first step into a realm where information, stories, and connections come alive on your screen.

When you first launch Safari, it greets you with a clean, intuitive interface that belies its underlying sophistication. The setup is straightforward, inviting you to start your journey with minimal fuss. It's like being handed the keys to a powerful vehicle; the design is sleek and the controls are easy to understand, yet under the hood lies a powerful engine ready to take you anywhere you wish to go on the web.

Your journey with Safari begins with familiarizing yourself with its basic features. The address bar at the top doubles as a search bar – a simple, yet ingenious design choice that streamlines your browsing experience. Here, you can type website URLs or queries directly, a feature that feels as natural as asking a question aloud. The moment you start typing, Safari springs into action, offering suggestions based on your input, predictive in its assistance, and keen in its responsiveness.

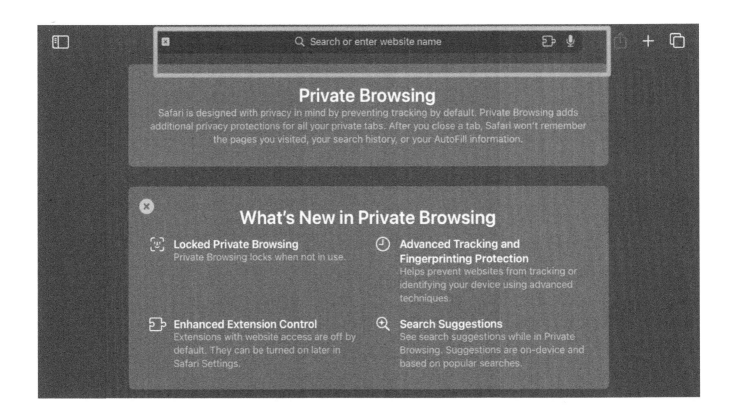

Tabs in Safari open up like pages in a book, allowing you to have multiple websites open simultaneously. You can easily switch between tabs, or open links in new tabs to keep your current page undisturbed. This feature is akin to having multiple books open on a desk, each one ready for your perusal at a moment's notice. Managing these tabs is effortless; you can reorder them, group them, or close them with simple gestures, keeping your browsing experience organized and fluid.

One of Safari's most significant features is its seamless integration with Apple's ecosystem. If you use Safari on other Apple devices, like an iPhone or a Mac, your browsing history, bookmarks, and even passwords can sync across all devices via iCloud. This synchronization is like having a personal assistant who remembers your preferences and needs, no matter where you are or what device you're using. It ensures a consistent browsing experience, one that is tailored to your habits and history.

Customizing Safari's settings allows you to tailor your browsing experience further. From choosing your preferred search engine to enabling features like pop-up blocking and warnings about fraudulent websites, these adjustments empower you to make Safari your own. It's akin to setting the rules of engagement for your web exploration, ensuring that your journey is safe, efficient, and aligned with your preferences.

The privacy features in Safari are also noteworthy. With Intelligent Tracking Prevention and the option to browse privately, Safari protects your browsing data, ensuring that your online activities remain your own. These features are akin to drawing the curtains in your home; they provide a space where you can explore and browse with the assurance of privacy and security.

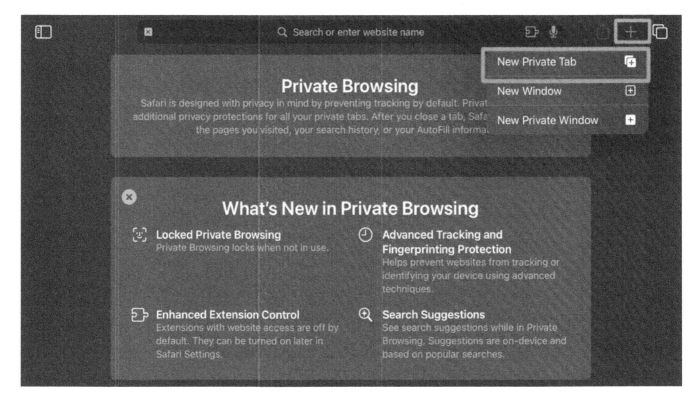

Setting up and using Safari on your iPad is the beginning of a journey that is both expansive and intimate. It opens up the world to you, offering a window to explore, learn, and connect. Yet, it also remains a deeply personal experience, one that respects your privacy and preferences. As you continue to explore the vast expanse of the web with Safari, it becomes more than a browser; it becomes a trusted companion on your digital journey, one that is both powerful and personal.

Searching the Web: Tips and Tricks

Navigating the vast ocean of information that is the internet can be akin to exploring uncharted waters; knowing how to search effectively is like having an expertly crafted map and a reliable compass. Searching the web from your iPad using Safari is a skill that combines art and science. It's about knowing how to phrase your queries, understanding the tools at your disposal, and using savvy techniques to reach the precise information you seek. This exploration of tips and tricks for searching the web is akin to acquiring navigational skills that ensure your digital voyage is both successful and efficient.

The first step in mastering web searches is understanding the art of query formulation. It's akin to knowing the right questions to ask in a conversation. Start by being specific in your search terms - the more precise your words, the more relevant your results. For instance, if you're looking for a recipe, include not just the dish name but also specific ingredients or dietary preferences. It's like telling a story where every detail contributes to the narrative, guiding Safari to deliver exactly what you need.

Another critical aspect of effective searching is the use of keywords and phrases. Keywords are the cornerstones of your queries, the pivotal points around which the search revolves. Think of them as the key ingredients in a recipe; without them, the final dish loses its distinct flavor. Phrases, on the other hand, are like binding these ingredients together. Using quotation marks to search for an exact phrase can dramatically narrow down your results to the most relevant pages.

The use of filters and advanced search options in Safari further refines your searching prowess. These tools are like a sieve, filtering out the irrelevant and keeping only the useful. You can filter results by date, type of content, or even language. Imagine having a set of fine brushes for an intricate painting – these tools allow you to bring out the finer details in the vast canvas of the web.

Knowing how to interpret and evaluate search results is also crucial. The top results are not always the most relevant or credible. It's important to scan through the first few results, read the descriptions, and decide which ones seem most pertinent. It's like scanning the horizon with a telescope; sometimes, what you need is not the nearest ship but the one that's heading in the right direction.

Utilizing the search suggestions offered by Safari can also be a valuable tactic. As you type, Safari proposes a list of potential completions to your query, based on popular searches and your past browsing history. These suggestions can be thought of as hints or clues, guiding you toward what you might be looking for, even before you fully articulate it.

Incorporating shortcuts and utilizing the voice search feature are like having secret passages and hidden tools that make your search journey more efficient. Voice search, in particular, offers a hands-free way to enter queries, especially useful when you're multitasking or if typing is inconvenient.

In essence, searching the web effectively on your iPad is a skill that blends precision, creativity, and a bit of intuition. It's about crafting your queries with care, using the right tools, and understanding how to sift through the sea of information to find the treasure you seek. As you hone these skills, every search becomes an adventure, a quest for knowledge where your iPad is both your compass and your map, guiding you to the riches of the web.

Setting Up Your Email

Setting up your email on the iPad is like establishing a digital home for your communications. It's a process that goes beyond mere technical setup; it's about creating a space where your conversations, connections, and correspondences can live and be managed with ease and efficiency. In the modern world, email remains a vital part of personal and professional life, and the iPad offers a seamless way to integrate this into your daily routine.

The journey of setting up your email begins with choosing an email provider. Whether you're using Apple's Mail app or a third-party application, the initial steps are designed to be intuitive and user-friendly. It's akin to selecting a new home; you decide which service best suits your needs, be it the simplicity and integration of iCloud, the widespread use of Gmail, or the professionalism of Outlook.

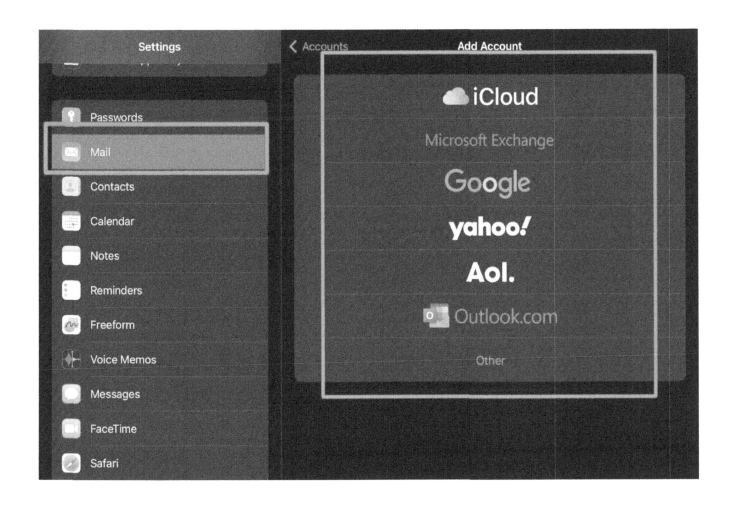

Entering your email credentials – your email address and password – is the key that unlocks your digital mailbox. This simple action is like turning a key in a lock, opening the door to a world of communication. The iPad's Mail app, with its clean and clear interface, then becomes a hub for your emails, organizing them into a coherent, easily navigable stream.

But setting up your email is more than just inputting credentials; it's about customizing the experience to fit your lifestyle. This involves adjusting settings such as fetch frequency, which determines how often your iPad checks for new emails. It's a choice that balances immediacy and convenience with the need to manage battery life and data usage. It's like setting the rhythm for your mail delivery, ensuring that you receive messages in a way that aligns with your daily schedule.

Organizing your inbox is another crucial aspect of setting up your email. Most email services and apps offer tools to categorize and prioritize messages, such as creating folders or marking important emails. This organization is similar to sorting mail into different trays or folders; it ensures that important communications are readily accessible, while less critical messages don't clutter your primary view.

Setting up notifications for your email is like installing a doorbell for your digital home. You decide which messages warrant immediate attention and notification. This customization means you're alerted to important emails as they arrive, while less urgent communications can wait until you choose to check your inbox.

For those with multiple email accounts, the iPad's email setup allows for easy switching between accounts, or even viewing all inboxes in a unified interface. It's like having multiple mailboxes with the convenience of one key that opens them all. This feature is particularly useful for those who juggle personal and professional emails or manage multiple roles.

In essence, setting up your email on the iPad is about creating a personalized communication center. It's a process that makes managing your digital conversations intuitive and efficient. As you go through this setup, your iPad becomes more than just a device; it becomes a companion in your communication journey, an integral part of your daily life where emails are not just received and sent but are managed in a way that suits your personal rhythm and style.

Sending and Receiving Emails

Mastering the art of sending and receiving emails on your iPad is akin to navigating the currents of modern communication, a journey that blends the timeless art of letter writing with the swift efficiency of digital technology. In this era, emails serve as a crucial bridge connecting various aspects of our personal and professional lives. The iPad, with its intuitive interface and robust capabilities, offers a seamless and enriching email experience, turning the act of sending and receiving emails into a harmonious blend of simplicity and sophistication.

When you compose an email on your iPad, it's like drafting a letter with a digital pen. The process begins with a tap on the compose button, a simple gesture that opens a blank canvas where your thoughts and words take shape. As you type, the virtual keyboard responds with tactile precision, each tap a building block in the construction of your message. The experience is as fluid and natural as writing on paper, yet empowered with digital tools that enhance and streamline your expression.

The act of sending an email is transformed into a swift and efficient process. Whether it's attaching a document from your files, inserting a photo from your gallery, or adding a link to a webpage, these actions are integrated seamlessly into the email composition. It's like having a desk with all your tools and resources within arm's reach, ready to be utilized as you craft your message. When you hit send, your words embark on a digital journey, delivered with speed and reliability that traditional mail could never match.

Receiving emails on your iPad is equally gratifying. Notifications alert you to new messages, a gentle nudge that respects your time and attention. Opening an email is like receiving a letter, each message a window into a conversation, an opportunity, or a piece of information. The Mail app organizes these messages efficiently, ensuring that your inbox remains a manageable and inviting space. It's like having a personal assistant who sorts your mail, presenting it to you in a coherent and orderly fashion.

The iPad's email interface is also adept at handling various types of content within emails. Whether it's viewing images, playing videos, or previewing documents, the experience is seamless and integrated. It's akin to having a multimedia communication device that brings content to life, making the act of reading an email a dynamic and interactive experience.

Moreover, managing email conversations on the iPad is a streamlined affair. The ability to flag important emails, categorize messages into folders, and search through conversations turns your inbox into an organized archive of communications. It's like having a filing system that's both intelligent and intuitive, one that adapts to your methods of organization and retrieval.

In essence, sending and receiving emails on the iPad elevates the experience of digital correspondence. It transforms a routine task into an enjoyable and efficient process, enriched by the iPad's responsive interface and powerful features. Whether you're composing a heartfelt message to a loved one, sending a professional proposal, or staying connected with friends and colleagues, the iPad ensures that your email experience is not just about communication, but about connection, clarity, and convenience. In your hands, the iPad becomes a powerful tool for correspondence, bridging distances and bringing people together in the vast digital landscape.

Managing Bookmarks and Favorites

In the digital odyssey of using your iPad, the ability to manage bookmarks and favorites in Safari is akin to charting your course through the vast seas of the internet. This functionality is not just a feature of convenience; it's a powerful tool for organizing the wealth of information and resources you encounter on your digital journeys. Managing bookmarks and favorites is like creating a personalized map of the online world, one that guides you back to the places that matter most, with efficiency and ease.

Imagine your Safari bookmarks as markers on a treasure map, each one leading you to a piece of digital gold that you have discovered and chosen to save. These could be articles that piqued your interest, websites you visit regularly for work or leisure, or online stores where you shop. Bookmarking these websites is a simple gesture – a tap on the share button and then 'Add Bookmark' – but it holds significant value. It's a way of saying, "This is important to me," and saving a piece of the digital universe for easy access later.

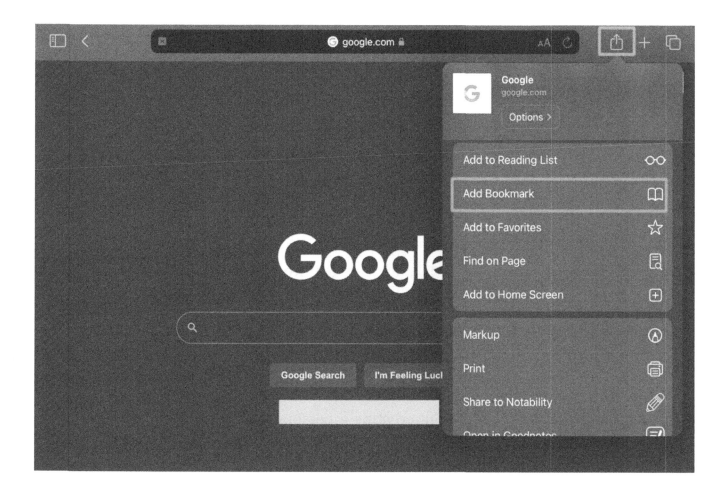

Organizing these bookmarks adds another layer to this personalized mapping. Safari allows you to create folders for your bookmarks, much like arranging books on shelves or files in a cabinet. This organization could be based on themes, such as 'Work', 'Recipes', 'News', or any other category that reflects your interests and activities. It's about creating order in the chaos of the internet, turning your bookmarks into a well-curated collection that's easily navigable.

Favorites, in Safari, hold a special place. These are the sites you want to have at your fingertips the moment you open a new tab. Adding a website to your Favorites is like pinning a location on your home map, declaring it as a frequently visited destination. Every time you open Safari or start a new tab, your Favorites are there, greeting you like the familiar sights of your neighborhood, ready to take you where you need to go with just a tap.

The process of managing these bookmarks and favorites is both intuitive and flexible. Safari's user-friendly interface makes it easy to edit, delete, or rearrange your bookmarks and favorites. Whether it's updating your list to reflect changing interests or keeping your most visited sites front and center, these changes are just a few taps away. It's akin to rearranging the furniture in your home for a fresh perspective or better functionality.

Furthermore, the sync functionality across Apple devices enhances the utility of bookmarks and favorites. If you use Safari on your iPhone or Mac, your bookmarks and favorites can be synchronized via iCloud. This feature ensures that the digital map you create is consistent across your devices, providing a seamless browsing experience whether you're on your iPad at home or checking your iPhone on the go.

In essence, managing bookmarks and favorites in Safari on your iPad is about more than just saving web addresses; it's about creating a personalized navigational system for the internet. It's a reflection of your interests, needs, and habits, a curated collection of digital destinations that are important to you. As you continue to explore the vast and ever-changing online world, these bookmarks and favorites become your compass and guide, ensuring that no matter where you roam in the digital space, you can always find your way back to the places that matter most.

Your iPad is now more than a device; it's a trusted companion on your digital voyage, adept at charting courses through the intricate networks of the online world.

Chapter 7. Communication Made Easy

Embarking on the journey of mastering communication on your iPad is akin to unlocking a treasure trove of connections and interactions. This realm of digital communication opens up avenues that blend the simplicity of traditional conversation with the marvels of modern technology. From the immediacy of FaceTime video calls to the thoughtful exchange of emails, and the dynamic world of social media, each aspect offers a unique way to stay connected. For seniors, especially, these tools are not just about keeping up with technology; they represent bridges to family, friends, and the global community. The joy of this journey lies in discovering the ease and accessibility with which these platforms bring loved ones closer, making every interaction both meaningful and enjoyable.

Making Video Calls with FaceTime

In the realm of modern communication, making video calls with FaceTime on your iPad is like opening a magical window that connects you to the world. This technology, once a figment of science fiction, is now a tangible reality, transforming the way we connect with friends, family, and colleagues. FaceTime is not merely a tool; it's a bridge that spans geographical divides, bringing us face-to-face with our loved ones and peers, irrespective of the miles that separate us.

Imagine stepping into a room where the walls are portals to different parts of the world. With just a few taps on your iPad, FaceTime enables these virtual meetings, creating experiences that are as close to real-life interactions as possible. The process of initiating a video call is incredibly straightforward, symbolizing Apple's commitment to user-friendly technology. You select a contact, tap the FaceTime icon, and within moments, you are greeted by the smiling face of a friend or a relative, a moment that defies distance and time zones.

The clarity and quality of FaceTime video calls are akin to looking through a clear, unblemished glass. Apple's continuous improvements in software and hardware ensure that the video and audio quality of your calls are crisp and steady. This clarity brings a sense of realism to your conversations, bridging the gap between virtual and physical presence. It's as if the person on the other end of the call is sitting across the table from you, making the experience deeply personal and engaging.

One of the most enchanting aspects of FaceTime is its ability to host group calls. This feature is like gathering friends and family into a living room for a reunion. Whether it's celebrating a birthday, holding a remote study group, or having a virtual get-together, group FaceTime calls can connect up to 32 people at once. Each face appears in a tile on the screen, creating a tapestry of smiling faces, laughter, and conversation, making distances feel inconsequential.

FaceTime also offers features that enhance the way we communicate beyond mere words. The use of Animoji and Memoji during calls adds a playful and creative element to conversations, allowing you to express yourself in fun and unique ways. These digital avatars mirror your facial expressions and movements, adding a layer of animation and personality to your interactions.

Moreover, FaceTime's integration with other Apple devices ensures seamless connectivity. Whether you're answering a call on your iPhone, continuing it on your iPad, or switching to your Mac, the transition is smooth and effortless. This interconnectedness signifies the versatility and adaptability of FaceTime, making it a reliable tool for communication in various scenarios and settings.

In essence, making video calls with FaceTime on your iPad is a celebration of human connection in the digital age. It epitomizes how technology can bring us closer, fostering relationships and creating moments that transcend physical barriers. As you use FaceTime, whether for casual chats or significant occasions, it becomes more than just a feature; it becomes a vital part of your life, enhancing communication and nurturing relationships in ways that were once deemed impossible.

Messaging with Friends and Family

In the tapestry of digital communication, messaging with friends and family using your iPad weaves a thread of intimacy and immediacy that transcends traditional barriers. This method of communication has evolved beyond the constraints of time and space, turning your iPad into a portal where conversations come alive, keeping you connected with those you hold dear. It's not just about exchanging words; it's about sharing life's moments, big and small, with the people who matter most.

The journey of messaging begins with the simplicity and versatility of the iPad's messaging apps. Whether you are using Apple's native Messages app or other popular platforms like WhatsApp or Facebook Messenger, each app provides a unique window for conversation. The Messages app, in particular, stands out for its seamless integration within the Apple ecosystem, offering a fluid and intuitive experience. It's akin to having a private conversation room that's always open, always ready for your next interaction.

The act of sending a message is as effortless as it is powerful. With a few taps, your thoughts, updates, and sentiments are instantly transmitted across the globe. It's akin to sending a digital letter, but one that arrives instantaneously, breaking down the waiting time that once characterized long-distance communication. This immediacy brings a sense of closeness, a feeling that no matter how far apart you are, your loved ones are just a message away.

Messaging is also about versatility in communication. The iPad's messaging platforms allow for more than just text; they enable you to send a wide array of multimedia – photos, videos, voice notes, and even drawings. This array of options adds color and depth to your conversations. Sending a photo of a new place, a video of a special event, or a voice note just to say hello adds a personal touch to your messages, making them feel more intimate and engaging.

Group messaging is another facet that enhances the experience. It's like gathering your family or friends in a virtual living room, where everyone can join the conversation, share news, and stay connected. Whether it's planning a family reunion, sharing updates, or just keeping up with each other's lives, group chats create a sense of community and belonging, keeping you intertwined with your social circle.

The convenience of messaging on the iPad is further amplified by features like speech-to-text, enabling you to compose messages using your voice. This feature is particularly beneficial when your hands are busy, or typing is inconvenient. It's like having a conversation where the iPad listens and transcribes your words into written messages, bridging the gap between spoken language and written communication.

Furthermore, messaging apps on the iPad offer various customization and privacy features, allowing you to tailor your messaging experience. From customizing notifications and chat backgrounds to managing privacy settings, these features ensure that your messaging experience aligns with your personal preferences and comfort level.

In essence, messaging with friends and family on the iPad is a dynamic and multifaceted form of communication. It combines the immediacy of real-time conversation with the richness of multimedia sharing, all within the palm of your hand. As you navigate this digital communication landscape, your iPad becomes more than just a device; it becomes a key player in maintaining and strengthening your relationships, bridging distances, and bringing your social world closer.

Using Social Media Safely

Navigating the vibrant landscape of social media on your iPad is akin to exploring a bustling digital city, filled with conversations, interactions, and a myriad of opportunities to connect. In this modern age, social media platforms like Facebook, Twitter, Instagram, and LinkedIn have become integral to our daily communications. They offer a window to the world, allowing us to share experiences, stay informed, and maintain relationships. However, venturing into this digital city requires more than just the ability to post and comment; it demands an awareness of safety, privacy, and responsible usage.

When you embark on your social media journey, think of it as setting out to explore a vast metropolis. Each platform is like a different district, each with its unique culture, norms, and modes of interaction. The first step is to understand the landscape. Familiarize yourself with the settings and features of each platform. Just as you would learn the roads and landmarks of a new city, learn how to navigate your social media settings. Adjust privacy controls to manage who can see your posts and interact with you. It's akin to choosing the right neighborhood to live in – one that feels safe, comfortable, and reflective of your lifestyle.

Engaging with others on social media should be like participating in a respectful public forum. It involves sharing your thoughts and experiences, but also listening and responding to others. As in any city, there are various voices and perspectives. Engage with empathy and consideration, understanding that behind every profile is a real person, with feelings and a story of their own. Practice discernment in what you share and how you interact. Just as you wouldn't disclose personal details to a stranger on the street, be cautious about the information you share online.

Staying safe on social media also means being aware of the digital footprints you leave behind. Every post, like, comment, and share contributes to your online persona – an identity that can have both personal and professional implications. Consider how your online actions reflect on you, much like how your behavior in a community reflects on your character. Be mindful of the permanence of your digital actions, as what is shared on the internet often stays there.

Beware of the pitfalls of social media, including misinformation, cyberbullying, and phishing scams. Just as a city has its hazards, so does the digital world. Learn to recognize and avoid these dangers. Verify information before you share it, be wary of suspicious links, and report any abusive behavior. Safeguarding your digital well-being is as crucial as taking care of your physical safety in a city.

Moreover, balance your social media use with real-life interactions. While these platforms provide valuable connections, they are but a complement to, not a substitute for, face-to-face relationships and experiences. It's important to periodically disconnect, to step back and enjoy the world beyond the screen. Just as one would take a break from the hustle and bustle of city life, so too should you take digital breaks, ensuring that your social media usage is balanced and healthy.

In essence, using social media safely on your iPad is about navigating this digital city with awareness, respect, and responsibility. It's about making connections, sharing experiences, and enriching your life, all while maintaining your safety, privacy, and well-being. As you explore this vibrant digital landscape, remember that the way you engage with social media can define your experience – turning it into either a fulfilling journey or a perilous venture.

Email Attachments and Photos

In the digital age, managing email attachments and photos on your iPad is akin to being an adept curator of a personal digital gallery. This task transcends the basic act of attaching and downloading files. It is about seamlessly integrating pieces of your digital life—photos, documents, videos—into your communications, making your interactions richer and more expressive. Handling email attachments and photos on the iPad is not just a functional necessity; it's an art form that enhances the narrative of your emails, turning each message into a more comprehensive and engaging story.

Imagine your email as a canvas, and attachments are the colors and textures you add to convey your message more vividly. The iPad, with its intuitive interface and robust capabilities, makes this process incredibly streamlined. Whether it's attaching a photo from your last vacation to share with family or sending an important document to a colleague, the ease with which you can add these files to your emails is reminiscent of an artist effortlessly selecting the perfect hues for their painting.

The process of attaching a file in an email is straightforward yet powerful. When composing an email, you're presented with the option to attach files with just a few taps. It's like opening a drawer filled with tools and choosing the right one for the task at hand. You can attach photos and videos from your gallery, documents from your iCloud Drive or other storage services, and even scan documents directly using your iPad's camera. Each attachment, whether a photo, a PDF, or a spreadsheet, adds a layer of depth to your message, transforming it from a simple text into a rich, multi-dimensional communication.

Receiving and downloading attachments is equally seamless. When an email arrives with an attached file, it's like receiving a package. You preview the attachment with a tap, and with another, you can save it to your desired location on your iPad. This process is akin to placing a received gift on your shelf, where it can be easily accessed and viewed. Whether it's a photo, a document, or any other type of file, handling these attachments is done with a level of ease and intuitiveness that makes the experience both enjoyable and efficient.

Organizing and managing these attachments is also an essential part of the process. The iPad's Files app acts like a digital filing cabinet, a place where you can store, organize, and access all your attachments. You can create folders, label them, and arrange your files just as you would in a physical file cabinet. This organization ensures that your digital life is orderly and manageable, making it easy to find and share attachments when needed.

Moreover, the integration of cloud storage services with the iPad's email functionality offers an additional layer of convenience and accessibility. Services like iCloud, Dropbox, or Google Drive allow you to access a wide array of files from anywhere, at any time. This connectivity ensures that your important documents and cherished photos are always within reach, ready to be shared or viewed.

In essence, handling email attachments and photos on your iPad is a multifaceted process that combines functionality with creativity. It's about more than just attaching files; it's about weaving these digital elements into the fabric of your communications, enriching your conversations, and keeping your digital life organized and accessible. As you master the art of managing these attachments and photos, your iPad becomes more than just a device; it becomes a powerful tool in your communication arsenal, one that brings your messages to life and keeps your digital world at your fingertips.

Keeping in Touch: Tips for Seniors

Navigating the digital landscape of communication can be a delightful and enriching journey for seniors, one that bridges generational gaps and opens doors to new forms of connection. The iPad, with its user-friendly interface and versatile capabilities, serves as an ideal companion for seniors embarking on this journey. Keeping in touch through this remarkable device is not merely about learning new technologies; it's about enhancing relationships, exploring the modern world of communication, and embracing the joy of staying connected with family, friends, and the broader community.

The first step in this adventure is embracing the simplicity and intuitiveness of the iPad. Its design, characterized by large, clear icons and a responsive touch screen, makes navigation straightforward. For seniors, this ease of use is like finding a book written in clear, large print, making the reading experience enjoyable and stress-free. The iPad thus becomes a friendly tool, one that invites exploration rather than intimidation.

FaceTime, Apple's video calling feature, is a marvel for seniors seeking visual connection with loved ones. Imagine being able to see the smiling faces of grandchildren, hear their laughter, and share stories as if you were sitting in the same room. FaceTime calls break down the barriers of distance, allowing for heartwarming interactions that are priceless. The process of making a FaceTime call is straightforward: with just a few taps, seniors can be face-to-face with their loved ones, sharing moments and creating memories.

Messaging and emailing on the iPad offer another layer of connectivity. These methods of communication are perfect for quick updates or sharing thoughts and photos. For seniors, sending a message or an email can be as easy as writing a letter, but with the immediacy and convenience that digital technology provides. This way, staying in the loop with family updates or reconnecting with old friends becomes a daily possibility rather than an occasional luxury.

Social media platforms can also be a gateway to expanded social circles and interests. Seniors can follow pages and groups that align with their hobbies and passions, connecting with like-minded individuals across the globe. Navigating social media safely is crucial, and with the iPad's intuitive settings, managing privacy and understanding online interactions can be learned and controlled effectively.

Another important aspect is organizing and personalizing the iPad to suit individual preferences. Seniors can customize their device by arranging apps and settings in a way that feels most natural and accessible to them. This personalization makes the iPad not just a tool, but a companion attuned to their unique needs and lifestyle.

In addition, embracing accessibility features of the iPad can transform the experience for seniors. Features like voice-to-text, larger text options, and Siri, the voice assistant, can be particularly beneficial. These features offer ways to interact with the device that don't rely solely on touch or sight, making the iPad a more inclusive and versatile device for seniors with varying abilities.

In essence, the iPad opens a world of communication possibilities for seniors, offering them ways to stay engaged, connected, and updated. By embracing these modern tools of communication, seniors are not only keeping up with the evolving world but are also enriching their lives with new forms of interaction and engagement. The iPad, in this respect, becomes more than a gadget; it becomes a window to the world, a facilitator of cherished relationships, and a testament to the timeless importance of staying connected.

Chapter 8. Enjoying Media and Entertainment

Embarking on the exploration of media and entertainment on your iPad is like opening a door to a world rich with sensory experiences and storytelling. This journey transforms your device into a versatile companion that entertains, informs, and engages. From capturing and reliving memories in photos, immersing in the diverse realms of music and podcasts, to getting lost in captivating movies and eBooks, each activity offers a unique flavor of enjoyment. The simplicity and interactivity of games add a playful touch, making the iPad a comprehensive source of digital amusement. This exploration is about more than just consumption; it's an active engagement with content that resonates, entertains, and enriches your daily life, offering new dimensions of enjoyment at your fingertips.

Photos: Capturing and Viewing

In the realm of media and entertainment on your iPad, the world of photography holds a special charm. The process of capturing and viewing photos on this device is not just a functional activity; it's an artistic endeavor that opens up a window to memories, emotions, and stories. The iPad, with its high-resolution camera and vivid display, turns every user into both a photographer and an audience, weaving a tapestry of visual storytelling that's rich in detail and emotion.

Imagine your iPad as a painter's canvas and the camera as your brush. Capturing photos is akin to painting with light and shadows. The simplicity with which you can point your device, frame a scene, and click to capture a moment is reminiscent of an artist's swift stroke that brings a scene to life. Whether it's a family gathering, a breathtaking landscape, or a candid street scene, each photo you take is a testament to your perspective, a frozen slice of time that tells a story.

The quality of the iPad's camera adds depth to this narrative. With features like high dynamic range (HDR) and image stabilization, each picture you take is not just a mere image but a vivid representation of the moment. The colors are vibrant, the details sharp, and the contrasts striking. It's like having a professional studio in your hands, where technology aids in bringing out the true essence of your subject.

But capturing photos is just one part of the journey. Viewing these photos on your iPad is an experience in itself. The device's retina display renders images in stunning clarity and color, turning each viewing into a private gallery exhibition. Swiping through your photo library is like walking through a gallery of your life, where each image evokes memories and emotions. The ability to zoom in and appreciate the finer details of a photo, or to view them as a slideshow, adds dynamism to your photo library, transforming it from a mere collection into a vivid storytelling medium.

Organizing and editing these photos further enhances the experience. The iPad's Photos app is not just a storage space; it's a dynamic tool where you can organize your memories into albums, highlight favorites, and even edit images to perfection. Adjusting the exposure, cropping to frame, applying filters – each edit you make is like adding your personal touch to the picture, refining the story it tells.

Sharing these photos brings yet another dimension of joy. Whether it's through social media, email, or instant messaging, sharing your pictures with friends and family is like opening the pages of your visual diary for others to read. It's a way of sharing your experiences, your joys, and your perspective with the world, bridging distances and creating connections through the power of imagery.

In essence, the process of capturing and viewing photos on your iPad is a celebration of visual storytelling. It's a blend of technology and artistry that enables you to not only preserve moments but to relive and share them in a way that's rich and engaging. Each picture you take and view on your iPad is more than just a pixelated image; it's a chapter of your life's story, rendered in vivid color and detail, waiting to be revisited and cherished.

Listening to Music and Podcasts

In the realm of media and entertainment on your iPad, listening to music and podcasts is akin to embarking on an auditory journey that transcends the boundaries of time and space. This experience is not just about passive listening; it's a rich engagement that weaves sound into the fabric of daily life, transforming mundane moments into something more profound and enjoyable. Your iPad becomes a personal concert hall or a discussion forum, offering an array of auditory experiences from the latest music albums to insightful podcasts on myriad topics.

The journey of listening to music on your iPad is like entering a vast musical library with endless aisles of albums and tracks. Whether you're a fan of classical symphonies, jazz improvisations, rock anthems, or contemporary pop hits, the iPad opens up a universe of music. With apps like Apple Music, Spotify, or Pandora, you have access to millions of songs at your fingertips. It's like having a ticket to the world's largest music festival, where every artist and genre is represented.

Listening to music on your iPad is an experience that can be both private and immersive. With a pair of headphones, you enter a personal sound space, where every note, chord, and beat resonates with clarity and emotion. The iPad's audio quality ensures that whether you're listening to the delicate nuances of a classical piece or the deep bass of a modern track, the sound is rich and true to life. It's an experience that's as intimate as listening to a musician play just for you in a cozy room.

Podcasts offer a different flavor in this auditory feast. They are like attending a series of intriguing lectures, engaging discussions, or storytelling sessions. The iPad's podcast app provides access to an expansive range of topics – from educational content and gripping true-crime stories to interviews with notable personalities and discussions on health and lifestyle. Each podcast is an opportunity to learn, to be entertained, or to gain new perspectives on various subjects.

The ease of accessing and organizing music and podcasts on the iPad adds to the enjoyment. Creating playlists of your favorite songs, downloading tracks for offline listening, or subscribing to podcast channels – all these actions are intuitive and straightforward. It's like curating your own personal collection of audio experiences, tailored to your tastes and preferences.

Moreover, the versatility of the iPad allows you to integrate music and podcasts into various aspects of your life. Whether it's listening to upbeat tracks during a workout, enjoying calming melodies while cooking, or catching up on a podcast during your commute, the iPad adapts to your lifestyle, providing a soundtrack that enhances your daily routine.

In essence, listening to music and podcasts on your iPad is a journey through a world of sound. It's a journey that entertains, informs, and accompanies you throughout your day. The iPad transforms from a mere gadget into a vessel of auditory exploration, bridging genres and topics, and connecting you to the vast world of music and spoken word. As you put on your headphones or play music through the speakers, each session becomes a moment of escape, discovery, and enjoyment – a testament to the power of sound in enriching our lives.

Watching Videos and Movies

Immersing yourself in the world of videos and movies on your iPad is akin to having a personal theater experience at your fingertips. This journey is about more than just viewing content; it's an exploration of diverse worlds, stories, and emotions, all conveyed through the vibrant display of your device. Your iPad transforms into a portal of cinematic wonder, where each video or movie becomes a window into different realities, cultures, and imaginations.

Picture your iPad as a canvas where filmmakers paint their stories in moving images. The high-resolution screen and exceptional sound quality bring these narratives to life with vivid detail and clarity. Whether you're watching a fast-paced action movie, a heartwarming drama, or a thought-provoking documentary, the iPad's display and audio immerse you in the experience. It's like having a front-row seat in a cinema, where the screen fills your field of vision and the sound envelopes you.

The convenience of streaming services on the iPad, such as Netflix, Hulu, or Disney+, offers an endless library of movies and videos. It's like having a film festival at your command, where you can choose from the latest releases, timeless classics, or niche indie films. This accessibility breaks down the barriers of traditional movie-watching, allowing you to explore content from around the world, each film a journey into a different culture or perspective.

The experience of watching videos and movies on the iPad is also about personalization. You can create watchlists, rate your favorite films, and receive recommendations based on your viewing history. It's akin to having a personal curator who understands your tastes and preferences, guiding you to your next great cinematic adventure. The iPad learns what you love, offering suggestions that align with your interests, ensuring that every viewing is as enjoyable as the last.

For those who love to dive deep into genres or directors, the iPad offers tools to explore and discover. You can search for films by theme, era, or style, making it easy to embark on a thematic journey through cinema history. It's like having a library where the books are arranged not just alphabetically, but also by their essence and spirit.

The flexibility of the iPad also enhances your movie-watching experience. You can watch a movie in one sitting or in parts, according to your schedule. The device's portability means you can enjoy films anywhere – curled up on your couch, during a flight, or in a cozy corner of a café. It's like carrying a personal movie theater wherever you go, one that adapts to your lifestyle.

Moreover, the iPad offers ways to share your movie experiences with others. Through features like AirPlay, you can stream movies to your Apple TV, turning your living room into a movie theater for family and friends. Sharing your favorite films or videos becomes a way of connecting with others, a shared experience that brings people together.

In essence, watching videos and movies on your iPad is a celebration of storytelling and visual art. Each viewing is an opportunity to escape, learn, feel, and connect. Your iPad becomes more than just a device; it transforms into a storyteller, a guide, and a companion in your cinematic journey, bringing the magic of movies into the palm of your hand.

Reading eBooks and News

In the landscape of media and entertainment on the iPad, the act of reading eBooks and news articles represents a delightful blend of the traditional charm of reading with modern digital convenience. This experience on your iPad is akin to having a vast, ever-expanding library at your fingertips, a library that not only stores volumes of literature and current affairs but also presents them in a format that's tailored to your reading preferences. Engaging with eBooks and news on your iPad is not just about consuming content; it's a journey through worlds crafted in words, enhanced by the interactive and customizable nature of digital media.

Imagine your iPad as a portal to literary realms and global events. The ability to read eBooks on this device is like having access to every book you've ever wanted to read, available instantaneously. Whether it's the latest bestseller, a classic novel, or an informative non-fiction work, the iPad brings these to you with ease. Apps like Apple Books, Kindle, or Kobo turn your device into a personal bookshelf, one that can hold thousands of books without occupying physical space. It's a bibliophile's dream, where the next story is just a tap away.

The experience of reading on the iPad is further enriched by the features that digital books offer. You can adjust the font size and style for comfortable reading, use the built-in dictionary to look up unfamiliar words, or even switch to the night mode to reduce eye strain. It's like having a book that automatically adjusts to your reading environment and preferences, ensuring that your immersion in the narrative is uninterrupted and complete.

Beyond the realms of fiction and literature, the iPad also serves as a window to the world through digital news. With apps for newspapers and magazines, as well as aggregators like Apple News, staying updated with current events is more accessible than ever. The layout and design of news articles on the iPad make the reading experience engaging, with interactive elements like embedded videos, audio clips, and infographics. It's akin to reading a dynamic newspaper that's constantly updated and personalized to your interests.

Moreover, the convenience of reading news on the iPad means you can stay informed anytime, anywhere. Whether it's catching up with the day's headlines over morning coffee, reading in-depth articles during your commute, or browsing through magazine features in the evening, the iPad adapts to your schedule. It's a continuous flow of information, presented in a format that's digestible and enjoyable.

The customization options extend to how you curate your news feed. You can follow specific topics, subscribe to particular magazines, or set up alerts for breaking news, tailoring the influx of information to your preferences and areas of interest. It's like having a newspaper that's designed just for you, with every section and article aligned with your curiosity and concerns.

In essence, reading eBooks and news on the iPad is more than just a digital iteration of traditional reading; it's an enhanced and personalized experience. It offers the joy of exploring stories and staying informed, enriched by the convenience, interactivity, and adaptability of digital media. Your iPad becomes a bridge to knowledge, stories, and insights, making the act of reading a delightful blend of entertainment, education, and enlightenment.

Playing Simple and Fun Games

In the diverse landscape of media and entertainment available on the iPad, playing simple and fun games stands out as a delightful avenue of joy and leisure. This aspect of the iPad experience is not merely a pastime; it's a vibrant world of interactive entertainment that offers relaxation, mental stimulation, and a playful escape from the everyday routine. For many, these games are a gentle foray into the digital gaming world, providing experiences that are both accessible and enjoyable without the complexities often associated with advanced gaming.

Imagine your iPad as a playful companion, one that holds a treasure trove of games ranging from classic puzzles to modern adventures. These games, with their user-friendly interfaces and engaging content, are akin to a collection of digital board games, card games, and brain teasers. Whether it's a quick round of solitaire, a strategic match in a puzzle game, or an immersive experience in a story-driven adventure, the iPad offers a variety of games to suit any mood and preference.

One of the joys of playing games on the iPad is the simplicity and intuitiveness of the experience. Games designed for the iPad often prioritize ease of use, making them accessible to players of all ages and skill levels. The touch screen interface adds a tactile dimension to gameplay, making interactions feel more natural and engaging. It's like returning to the simplicity of childhood games, but with a digital twist that adds a new layer of fun and interactivity.

The variety of games available on the iPad ensures that there's something for everyone. For those who enjoy a mental challenge, puzzle games offer a way to exercise the brain, with levels that progressively increase in difficulty. For those seeking relaxation, there are games with serene settings and calming gameplay, perfect for unwinding after a long day. The iPad also offers educational games, which combine learning and fun, making them a great choice for younger users or anyone interested in playful learning.

Another wonderful aspect of gaming on the iPad is the ability to connect with others. Many games offer multiplayer options, allowing you to play with friends and family, whether they are in the same room or across the globe. This social element transforms gaming from a solitary activity into an opportunity for bonding and shared enjoyment. It's like gathering around a board game on a family night, but with the flexibility and variety that digital games provide.

For seniors and those not typically inclined towards gaming, the iPad's simple games can be a delightful discovery. These games are not overwhelming; instead, they offer gentle entertainment and a chance to engage with technology in a fun and positive way. Playing games on the iPad can also be beneficial for cognitive health, offering an enjoyable way to keep the mind active and sharp.

In essence, playing simple and fun games on the iPad is an experience that combines entertainment, mental stimulation, and social interaction. It's a world where digital play is accessible and enjoyable, where games are not about competition or skill, but about enjoyment, relaxation, and the pure pleasure of play. As you explore the variety of games available on your iPad, you'll find that they add a playful dimension to your digital experience, turning your device into a source of joy and a gateway to lighthearted entertainment.

These experiences transform the iPad from a mere gadget into a source of endless exploration and joy, enhancing the routines of daily life with moments of pleasure, learning, and relaxation. The iPad thus stands as a testament to the power of technology in enriching our lives with a wide array of media and entertainment options, bringing the world to our fingertips in vivid color and sound.

Chapter 9. Practical Applications for Everyday Use

Embarking on a journey through the practical applications of your iPad unveils a world where technology seamlessly integrates into the fabric of daily life. This exploration reveals how the iPad becomes an essential companion, enhancing productivity and personal organization. From orchestrating your day with the Calendar, managing tasks through Reminders, to the thoughtful compilation of ideas in Notes, each application plays a pivotal role in streamlining your routine. Delving further, the Maps app opens pathways to exploration and discovery, while health apps encourage a focus on personal wellness. This journey through the iPad's practical applications is about harnessing the power of technology to make everyday tasks more manageable, efficient, and attuned to your lifestyle, transforming ordinary moments into opportunities for organization and self-improvement.

Calendar for Organizing Your Day

In the dynamic world of managing personal and professional life, the Calendar app on your iPad emerges as a cornerstone of organization. This application is not just a digital version of a traditional calendar; it's a sophisticated tool that helps orchestrate your daily activities, transforming the iPad into a personal planner and assistant. Utilizing the Calendar app is like having a personal secretary who keeps track of your schedule, reminds you of appointments, and helps you navigate the complexities of modern life's time demands.

Imagine your day as a tapestry of events, tasks, and appointments, each with its unique time and place. The Calendar app on your iPad weaves this tapestry, creating a structured and coherent picture of your day. It begins with the simplicity of adding events. Whether it's a business meeting, a doctor's appointment, a family gathering, or a personal reminder, adding these to your calendar is as easy as a few taps. You input the details: the what, where, and when, and the Calendar assimilates this information, turning it into an organized schedule.

One of the app's most remarkable features is its intuitive interface. The visual layout of the calendar – be it daily, weekly, or monthly view – provides a clear and comprehensive overview of your schedule. This visualization is akin to having a map of your time, where you can easily see how your day or week is structured at a glance. It's about transforming abstract time into a tangible, manageable construct.

The Calendar app also excels in customization and flexibility. You can color-code different types of events, making it easy to distinguish between work-related activities, personal appointments, or social events at a glance. This color-coding is like using different colored pens in a physical planner, a method that is not only functional but also aesthetically pleasing.

Moreover, the app's integration with other iOS devices ensures that you are always in sync. An appointment added on your iPad appears on your iPhone or Mac, keeping your schedule consistent across all devices. This feature ensures that no matter which device you're using, you're always up-to-date with your commitments. It's like having a planner that automatically updates itself, ensuring you're always informed.

Setting up alerts and reminders in the Calendar app is another crucial feature. These notifications are like gentle nudges, ensuring that you never miss an important event or task. You can customize these alerts to suit your preference, choosing when you want to be reminded – a day before, an hour before, or just at the moment. These reminders act as safety nets in your busy life, helping you stay on top of your commitments.

The Calendar app is also an excellent tool for managing invitations and RSVPs. You can send invitations to events from the app and receive notifications when someone accepts or declines. This feature makes organizing group events, meetings, or gatherings effortless and efficient.

In essence, the Calendar app on your iPad is more than a digital agenda; it's a comprehensive tool that brings order and clarity to your daily life. It helps you manage your time effectively, keeping track of your commitments and reminding you of them. The Calendar app turns your iPad into a valuable ally in navigating the busy waters of modern life, ensuring that you're always at the helm, in control of your time and activities.

Reminders: Never Forget Important Tasks

In the bustling rhythm of modern life, the Reminders app on your iPad emerges as a beacon of organization and efficiency. This tool is far more than a simple checklist; it's a dynamic system designed to ensure that your tasks, goals, and obligations are remembered and achieved. The Reminders app turns your iPad into a personal assistant, one that's meticulous, unobtrusive, and always at the ready. It's about transforming the daunting sea of tasks into manageable streams, ensuring that nothing important slips through the cracks of a busy schedule.

Imagine each task or obligation as a thread in the intricate fabric of your daily life. The Reminders app helps in weaving these threads together, creating a tapestry that is orderly and coherent. Adding a reminder is an effortless process: whether it's a grocery list, a work deadline, or a reminder to call a friend, you can quickly input the task and set a specific time for the alert. It's like planting a digital flag at a point in your future, one that you will eventually reach.

One of the most significant advantages of the Reminders app is its ability to categorize and prioritize tasks. You can create different lists for various aspects of your life – work, home, personal projects – and add tasks accordingly. This categorization is akin to organizing tasks into different drawers; each drawer contains items related to a specific area of your life, making it easy to focus and retrieve what you need without getting overwhelmed.

Customization is a key feature of the Reminders app, offering a variety of ways to tailor alerts to your personal routine. You can set reminders to be date-based, location-based, or even person-based. Imagine setting a reminder that triggers when you leave the office or when you arrive at the supermarket. These location-based reminders are like having a vigilant companion who gently nudges you when you're in the right place at the right time.

The integration of the Reminders app with Siri, Apple's voice assistant, adds another layer of convenience. You can dictate a reminder to Siri, turning a spoken sentence into a scheduled task. This feature is particularly useful when you're on the go, or when it's inconvenient to type. It's like having a secretary who is always listening, ready to note down your tasks at a moment's notice.

Additionally, the Reminders app is designed to work in harmony with other Apple devices. A reminder set on your iPad can show up on your iPhone or Mac, ensuring you're alerted regardless of which device you're currently using. This seamless synchronization means that your reminders follow you, not the other way around.

The app also supports sharing and collaboration, allowing you to share lists and tasks with family, friends, or colleagues. Coordinating on shared projects or planning a family event becomes much simpler when everyone involved has access to the same list of tasks and can contribute or tick off items in real time.

In essence, the Reminders app on your iPad is an indispensable tool in the art of task management. It's a system that's both simple and sophisticated, capable of handling the variety and complexity of modern life's demands. With the Reminders app, forgotten tasks and missed deadlines become a thing of the past, replaced by a sense of control and accomplishment. Your iPad, armed with this app, becomes more than just a device; it becomes a cornerstone of your daily organization, ensuring that you stay on top of your tasks and goals.

Notes: Taking and Organizing Notes

In the landscape of practical applications on your iPad, the Notes app stands as a testament to the art of simplicity in organization and creativity. This application is not just a digital notepad; it is a versatile tool that caters to a myriad of everyday needs - from jotting down quick ideas to compiling detailed research. Using the Notes app is akin to having a stack of notebooks, each customizable for a different purpose, all within the sleek frame of your iPad. It transforms your device into a personal scribe, where thoughts, ideas, and information are captured, organized, and accessed with ease and efficiency.

Imagine each note as a canvas where your thoughts and ideas take shape. Whether you're drafting a grocery list, outlining a novel, or capturing minutes of a meeting, the Notes app offers the flexibility to accommodate various types of content. The ease with which you can type, scribble, or even dictate your thoughts is reminiscent of a conversation with an old friend - natural, comfortable, and free-flowing. The app's ability to recognize and categorize handwritten notes further enhances its appeal, making it a perfect blend of traditional note-taking and modern technology.

One of the crowning features of the Notes app is its organizational capabilities. You can create separate notebooks for different projects or aspects of your life, much like having a shelf of labeled binders. Each notebook can be further organized with titles, headings, and bullet points, making the retrieval of information as straightforward as flipping through a well-organized file. This level of organization transforms the app into an extension of your memory, a place where information is not only stored but is also easily accessible.

The integration of multimedia into notes adds another dimension to this app. You can embed photos, sketches, web links, and even document scans within your notes. This feature turns each note into a comprehensive record, where visual cues accompany textual information, enhancing understanding and recall. It's like compiling a scrapbook for each project or idea, where every element is a piece of the bigger picture.

Collaboration in the Notes app is as simple as it is effective. You can share notes with colleagues, friends, or family, allowing for real-time collaboration. Whether it's a shared grocery list or a collaborative project plan, the app keeps everyone on the same page. This collaborative feature is akin to working on a communal blackboard, where everyone contributes, edits, and evolves ideas together.

Moreover, the search functionality in the Notes app is a powerful tool. You can quickly search for keywords or phrases across all your notes, making it easy to find the information you need without the hassle of manually flipping through pages. It's like having a personal assistant who knows exactly where everything is stored and can retrieve it in an instant.

In essence, the Notes app on your iPad is much more than a simple tool for jotting down thoughts. It's a sophisticated system for capturing, organizing, and sharing information. It adapts to your needs, whether you're a student, a professional, or someone who loves keeping their thoughts and ideas in order. The Notes app turns your iPad into a digital journal, planner, and archive, all rolled into one, making it an indispensable tool in your everyday life.

Maps: Getting Directions and Exploring

In the journey of everyday life, the Maps app on your iPad serves as an invaluable guide, providing directions and aiding exploration in a world that is increasingly connected yet complex. The utility of this app goes beyond mere navigation; it is a comprehensive tool that weaves together detailed maps, real-time traffic updates, and personalized location services. Utilizing the Maps app on your iPad is akin to having a knowledgeable local guide and an experienced navigator, all encapsulated within your digital device.

Imagine setting off on a journey, whether to a familiar destination or venturing into unknown territory. The Maps app is your companion, providing turn-by-turn directions that are both accurate and easy to follow. It's like having a compass that not only points north but also guides you through every turn, intersection, and roundabout. The app's voice-guided navigation ensures that your focus remains on the road, offering reassurance and clarity as you traverse the paths ahead.

The Maps app does more than just guide you from point A to point B; it enhances the journey itself. With detailed and interactive maps, you gain a bird's eye view of your surroundings. Streets, landmarks, and natural features are rendered in stunning detail, giving you a comprehensive understanding of the area. This feature transforms your iPad into a window to the world, offering a panoramic view that enriches your understanding of the places you travel through.

One of the most dynamic features of the Maps app is its real-time traffic information. This tool is like having a lookout point at every corner, providing updates on traffic conditions, road closures, and estimated travel times. This information is invaluable in planning your routes, helping you avoid traffic jams, and ensuring that your journey is as efficient as possible.

Exploring new places is also a delight with the Maps app. The app's search functionality allows you to discover restaurants, shops, parks, and other points of interest. It's like having a directory of every city at your fingertips. Whether you're looking for a place to dine, a park to relax in, or a museum to visit, the Maps app points you in the right direction, complete with ratings, reviews, and photos contributed by other users.

For those who love to walk or cycle, the Maps app offers routes tailored to these modes of travel. It's like having a personalized guide that understands your preference for scenic paths or bike lanes. These routes not only direct you to your destination but also enhance the journey with beautiful landscapes and suitable paths.

Additionally, the Maps app's integration with public transportation systems in various cities around the world makes it an invaluable tool for urban commuters. Timetables, transit routes, and walking directions to stations are all available within the app. It's akin to having a timetable for every bus, train, and ferry in your pocket, simplifying the complexity of public transport.

In essence, the Maps app on your iPad is a multifaceted tool that caters to various aspects of navigation and exploration. It's more than just a digital map; it's a companion that guides, informs, and enriches your journeys. Whether you are navigating the daily commute, exploring a new city, or planning a road trip, the Maps app transforms your iPad into an essential travel companion, ensuring that every journey you undertake is well-informed and enjoyable.

Health Apps: Tracking Wellness

In the contemporary era where health and wellness have become paramount, the iPad emerges as a vital tool in managing and understanding personal well-being. The integration of health apps on this device transcends the traditional approach to health tracking. It's not just about recording data; it's a holistic journey towards understanding, maintaining, and enhancing one's health. These apps transform your iPad into a personal health coach, a digital diary of wellness, and a source of motivation and insight.

Picture the health apps on your iPad as the pieces of a puzzle that, when put together, provide a complete picture of your health. From monitoring physical activity and nutrition to tracking sleep patterns and heart rate, these apps gather data that is crucial to understanding your body's needs and responses. It's like having a personal health record that is constantly updated, giving you insights into the most intricate aspects of your well-being.

One of the key components of these health apps is their ability to track physical activity. Whether it's counting steps, recording workouts, or monitoring the intensity of physical exercises, these apps make keeping track of your fitness journey effortless. They work silently in the background, collecting data as you move through your day. This feature is like having a silent trainer who is always with you, observing, recording, and encouraging you towards your fitness goals.

Nutrition tracking is another significant facet of these health apps. They allow you to record your daily food intake, offering insights into your dietary habits. You can log meals, track macros and micronutrients, and even get suggestions for healthier eating choices. It's akin to having a nutritionist in your pocket, one that helps you understand the impact of your dietary choices on your overall health.

Sleep tracking is an increasingly popular feature in health apps. By monitoring your sleep patterns, these apps provide valuable data on the quality and quantity of your sleep. Understanding your sleep cycles is like deciphering a hidden aspect of your health, offering clues to improve the rest you get each night. It's a step towards recognizing the profound impact of sleep on your overall health and well-being.

Heart rate monitoring is another critical aspect. With the ability to track your heart rate over time, these apps give you insights into your cardiovascular health. This monitoring is like having a stethoscope that's always listening, providing real-time data that can be crucial for early detection of potential health issues.

Beyond tracking and recording data, these health apps also offer educational content, personalized recommendations, and goal-setting features. They're like having a library of health information at your fingertips, coupled with a personal advisor who helps you set and achieve realistic health objectives.

The integration of these health apps with other devices, like wearable fitness trackers or smartwatches, enhances their utility. This interconnected ecosystem of devices works in harmony, offering a more comprehensive view of your health.

In essence, health apps on your iPad represent a new age of personalized healthcare. They empower you with knowledge, offer insights into your health, and encourage a proactive approach to wellness. These apps are more than just digital tools; they are partners in your journey towards a healthier, more informed lifestyle. With every piece of data they gather and every insight they provide, they help you navigate the complex world of health and wellness, making the journey an integral part of your daily life.

Chapter 10. Troubleshooting Common Problems

Venturing into the realm of troubleshooting common problems with your iPad is an essential aspect of harnessing its full potential. This journey is about more than just quick fixes; it's about understanding the intricacies of your device and learning how to maintain its optimal performance.

Solving Wi-Fi Connectivity Issues

In the digital era, where connectivity is akin to a lifeline, encountering Wi-Fi issues on your iPad can feel like being stranded in a technological desert. Troubleshooting Wi-Fi connectivity problems, therefore, is not just about restoring internet access; it's about reconnecting you to the digital world. This journey of resolving Wi-Fi issues on your iPad involves understanding the nuances of wireless networks and applying practical solutions to re-establish and strengthen your connection to the web.

The first step in this troubleshooting expedition is akin to diagnosing a patient: identifying the symptoms and understanding the root cause. When your iPad fails to connect to Wi-Fi, it could manifest as an inability to find networks, persistent disconnection, or slow internet speeds. These problems might stem from various sources – your iPad, the router, the internet service, or external interference.

Begin by examining the most direct connection: your iPad's Wi-Fi settings. Ensuring that Wi-Fi is turned on and that you're trying to connect to the correct network may seem basic, but sometimes, solutions lie in simple checks. It's like ensuring that the power cord of an appliance is plugged in before seeking more complex repairs. Sometimes, toggling the Wi-Fi off and on can reinitiate the connection process, acting as a soft reset for network issues.

If the issue persists, delve deeper by examining the strength of the Wi-Fi signal. Weak signals could be due to physical obstructions or distance from the router. It's akin to trying to have a conversation across a crowded room; moving closer or removing barriers can make a significant difference. If possible, reposition your router to a more central location in your home or office, reducing the number of walls or large objects the signal must traverse.

Another effective strategy is to forget the Wi-Fi network on your iPad and reconnect as if it were a new network. This process clears any existing settings or issues that might have been causing the connection problem. Think of it as starting a new chapter in a book after finding a page full of errors; you're essentially beginning afresh, with the hope of a smoother experience.

Router-related issues are also a common culprit. Restarting your router can resolve a multitude of network problems. This action is similar to rebooting your iPad; it gives the router a chance to refresh its settings and clear any glitches. If your router has been operational for a prolonged period, a simple restart can often breathe new life into your Wi-Fi connectivity.

In cases where multiple devices struggle to connect, the problem might lie with your internet service provider. Contacting them can provide insights into larger network issues or outages in your area. It's like checking if the whole neighborhood is without electricity before concluding that your house's wiring is at fault.

For persistent problems, updating your router's firmware can be a solution. Firmware updates often include fixes for connectivity issues and improvements in performance. This process is akin to updating the operating system on your iPad; it ensures that your router is equipped with the latest software to perform optimally.

In essence, solving Wi-Fi connectivity issues on your iPad is a multi-faceted process that involves a combination of practical steps and a bit of detective work. It's about systematically eliminating potential issues until you find the root cause and can implement an effective solution. Restoring your Wi-Fi connection reinstates your link to the digital world, ensuring that your online activities, whether for work, entertainment, or communication, remain uninterrupted and fluid.

Managing App Crashes and Freezes

In the world of technology, encountering app crashes and freezes on your iPad can be a frustrating roadblock, akin to hitting an unexpected detour in a smooth journey. These disruptions, while common, require a keen understanding and a methodical approach to troubleshooting. Addressing app crashes and freezes is not merely about getting an app running again; it's about restoring the seamless and efficient performance that iPad users cherish. This task involves delving into the heart of your iPad's functionality, identifying the causes of these issues, and implementing solutions to ensure a stable and smooth experience.

The first step in tackling app crashes and freezes is akin to being a detective at a crime scene: identifying the culprit. Is it a specific app that consistently misbehaves, or is the issue widespread across multiple applications? This distinction is crucial. If a single app is the source of trouble, the issue might be with the app itself. It's like having a troublesome cog in a well-oiled machine; fixing or replacing it can restore the entire system's efficiency.

If you've pinpointed a specific app, the initial remedy is straightforward yet effective – restarting the app. This process is akin to resetting a puzzle; it gives the app a fresh start, clearing temporary glitches. To restart, double-click the Home button (or use the app switcher gesture on newer iPad models) to bring up the list of recent apps, swipe up on the problematic app to close it, and then reopen it. Often, this simple action can resolve minor crashes or freezes.

For persistent issues with a particular app, the next step is to check for updates. App developers frequently release updates to fix bugs and improve performance. Updating an app is like renewing its health certificate, ensuring it's equipped to function correctly. Access the App Store, find the app, and tap 'Update' if available. This step can often resolve ongoing issues as developers work to optimize their apps continuously.

Another effective strategy is to delete and reinstall the app. This action is more like a surgical procedure, removing the app entirely and replacing it with a fresh, uncorrupted version. Deleting the app clears all associated data, which might include corrupt files causing the issue. Reinstalling the app then provides a clean slate for its operation.

If the problem is more systemic, affecting multiple apps, the approach shifts. A good starting point is to check the iPad's storage. Insufficient storage space can lead to performance issues, as apps struggle to save data or function correctly. Managing your storage is akin to organizing a cluttered room; freeing up space can lead to a more efficient and orderly environment. You can check your iPad's storage in the Settings app and delete unnecessary files or apps to create more space.

Restarting your iPad can also resolve system-wide issues. This process is like rebooting a complex machine; it clears the memory and resets the operating system, potentially resolving underlying issues causing apps to crash or freeze. To restart, hold down the power button, slide to power off, and then turn the iPad back on after a few moments.

In cases where crashes and freezes persist, resetting all settings on your iPad can be a more drastic but effective solution. This step is similar to restoring factory settings; it returns your iPad's settings to their original state without deleting your data and apps. It can resolve deeper issues related to system configurations and preferences that might be causing instability.

In essence, managing app crashes and freezes on your iPad involves a blend of simple fixes, regular maintenance, and more thorough solutions when needed. It's about maintaining the harmony between the software and the powerful hardware of your iPad, ensuring a smooth, efficient, and enjoyable experience. Each step taken to resolve these issues not only restores functionality but also reinforces the reliability and user-friendly nature of the iPad, making it a dependable tool in your digital life.

Battery Life: Maximizing and Troubleshooting

In the realm of mobile technology, the battery life of your iPad is akin to the heartbeat of your device, vital for its sustained operation and performance. Troubleshooting battery life issues, therefore, is not just about keeping your device powered up; it's about ensuring that your digital companion is ready and able whenever you need it. This task requires a blend of proactive strategies to maximize battery longevity and insightful troubleshooting to address any drain issues, making it a crucial aspect of maintaining your iPad's health and efficiency.

Understanding the nuances of battery usage is the first step in this journey. Like a car's fuel consumption that varies with driving habits, your iPad's battery life is influenced by how you use the device. Screen brightness, background app refresh, and active connectivity (like Bluetooth and Wi-Fi) are among the primary factors that affect battery life. It's about finding a balance between functionality and power efficiency. Lowering the screen brightness, for instance, can significantly conserve battery life, similar to turning off unnecessary lights in a room to save electricity.

Another aspect of maximizing battery life is managing the apps that are active or running in the background. Some apps, especially those that frequently update content or use location services, can drain the battery faster than others. This situation is like having appliances in your home that consume more energy. Regularly closing apps that you are not using and disabling background app refresh for non-essential apps can help in reducing this drain. It's akin to unplugging devices that are not in use.

Updating to the latest version of iOS can also play a crucial role in battery management. With each update, Apple often introduces new battery-saving features and fixes for known issues that might be affecting battery life. Keeping your iPad updated is like ensuring your vehicle's engine is tuned up; it helps in running your device more efficiently.

When facing significant battery drain issues, checking the Battery Health feature is a wise move. This tool, found in the iPad's settings, gives you an insight into your battery's capacity and peak performance capability. It's like getting a health check-up for your battery, understanding its condition, and whether it can still hold the charge as it used to when it was new.

If the battery health is degraded, it might be time to consider a battery replacement, especially if the device is a few years old. A battery replacement can breathe new life into your iPad, similar to replacing an old battery in a car. However, it's important to seek professional assistance for this, preferably from an authorized Apple service provider.

For those times when you need to ensure your battery lasts as long as possible, employing power-saving measures can be invaluable. Activating Low Power Mode, for instance, is like putting your device on a power diet, where it conserves energy by limiting background activity and automatic downloads.

In cases where battery issues persist despite all efforts, it might indicate a more complex problem with the device. In such instances, consulting with Apple Support or visiting an Apple Store can provide the necessary technical assistance. It's akin to visiting a specialist when a general health check doesn't resolve an issue.

In essence, managing and troubleshooting battery life issues on your iPad is a critical aspect of your device's maintenance. It's about adopting practices that prolong battery life, being vigilant about apps and features that drain power, and taking corrective action when needed. A well-maintained battery ensures that your iPad remains a reliable and efficient tool in your daily life, always ready to support your digital needs.

Updating iOS: Why and How

The process of updating the iOS on your iPad is akin to giving your device a new lease on life. This crucial aspect of iPad maintenance ensures that your device is not only equipped with the latest features but also fortified with essential security updates. Understanding why and how to update iOS is not merely about keeping up with technological advancements; it's about ensuring that your iPad operates at its optimum, providing a secure, efficient, and enhanced user experience.

The 'why' of updating iOS can be likened to the reasons for regularly servicing a car. Just as a car needs periodic maintenance to run smoothly and safely, your iPad requires iOS updates for several key reasons. Firstly, these updates often include critical security patches that protect your device from vulnerabilities. In the digital world, where security threats are ever-evolving, these updates act as vital shields, safeguarding your personal information from potential breaches.

Moreover, iOS updates frequently introduce new features and improvements to existing ones. These additions are like upgrades to a car's features, enhancing its performance and comfort. Whether it's refining the user interface, adding new functionalities, or improving the efficiency of apps, each update enriches your iPad experience, making your interaction with the device more enjoyable and productive.

The updates also play a significant role in bug fixes. Every software has its quirks and issues, and iOS is no exception. Regular updates address these bugs, resolving issues that users may have encountered in previous versions. This process is similar to fixing mechanical issues in a vehicle, ensuring that everything runs smoothly and as expected.

When it comes to the 'how' of updating iOS, the process is designed to be user-friendly and straightforward, akin to a guided path that leads you through the update process. The first step is to ensure that your iPad is connected to a Wi-Fi network and has sufficient battery life, or is plugged into a power source. This preparation is like ensuring you have enough fuel and all the necessary tools before embarking on a journey.

The actual process of updating iOS can be initiated from your iPad's settings. Navigating to the General settings and then to Software Update presents you with information about the available iOS update. This step is akin to reading about the enhancements and repairs that a new car model offers over your current one.

The download and installation of the update are just a few taps away. Once you select 'Download and Install,' the iPad takes over the task. This part of the process is like handing over your car to a trusted mechanic; the device, much like a skilled technician, knows precisely what to do. The iPad will download the update, prepare it for installation, and then install it, sometimes requiring a restart to complete the process.

It's important to note that, during the update, your iPad might be temporarily unusable. This downtime is similar to waiting for a car's servicing to be complete; it's a necessary pause to ensure that everything is set up correctly.

In instances where your iPad isn't showing an available update, or if the update process encounters issues, Apple Support provides resources and assistance. Seeking help in such situations is like consulting a mechanic when a car's check engine light comes on; it's about getting expert help to address complex issues.

In summary, updating iOS on your iPad is a critical practice for maintaining the device's health, security, and functionality. Regular updates ensure that your iPad remains a robust, secure, and enjoyable tool, equipped to handle the demands of modern digital life. This process, integral to the iPad experience, ensures that your device stays current, secure, and as functional as possible.

When to Seek Help: Apple Support and Beyond

Navigating the complexities of technology can sometimes be akin to exploring an intricate labyrinth – while many paths can be tread alone, there are moments when a guide is necessary. In the context of using an iPad, understanding when and how to seek help is as crucial as troubleshooting the issues themselves. This understanding transforms the potentially daunting prospect of dealing with technical problems into a manageable, even empowering, part of the user experience. Seeking help from Apple Support and beyond is not an admission of defeat; it's a strategic step towards finding solutions and expanding your tech-savviness.

The decision to seek help hinges on the nature and severity of the issue at hand. For straightforward problems, such as basic functionality queries or common glitches, the first line of inquiry often lies within the iPad's resources, like the Tips app or the built-in user guide. This approach is like consulting the manual of a complex appliance; it empowers you to solve the problem with guidance from the manufacturer.

However, when the issue transcends basic troubleshooting – perhaps a persistent software bug, hardware malfunction, or a complex technical hitch – turning to Apple Support is a wise move. This step is akin to seeking a specialist when a general practitioner's advice doesn't suffice. Apple's support ecosystem is vast, ranging from online resources and community forums to direct assistance through phone, chat, or in-person appointments at an Apple Store.

One of the key factors in seeking help is the timeliness of the issue. If a problem significantly hinders your ability to use your iPad effectively, prompt action is essential. Delaying could exacerbate the issue or disrupt your usage further. This situation is like addressing a minor leak before it becomes a flood; timely intervention can prevent larger problems down the line.

For issues related to software, such as iOS glitches, app malfunctions, or syncing problems, online resources like Apple's support website or dedicated forums can be invaluable. These platforms are akin to libraries filled with specific case studies and solutions. Often, the challenge you're facing might have been encountered and resolved by others, and their experiences can guide you to a solution.

In cases of hardware-related problems – like a malfunctioning screen, unresponsive buttons, or battery issues – professional assessment is typically necessary. Apple's authorized service providers possess the expertise and tools to diagnose and repair hardware issues accurately. This step is similar to taking a car to a certified mechanic; it ensures that your device is in capable and qualified hands.

Knowing the warranty status of your iPad is also crucial when seeking help. If your device is still under warranty, or if you have AppleCare+, you might be eligible for covered or reduced-cost services. This knowledge is like understanding an insurance policy; it helps you make informed decisions about repairs and services.

Lastly, never underestimate the power of community knowledge. Forums like Apple's support community or other tech forums can be goldmines of information, where experienced users and tech enthusiasts share advice and solutions. Engaging with these communities is like joining a study group; it's a collaborative effort to learn and solve problems.

In essence, knowing when and how to seek help for iPad issues is a critical component of the user experience. It's about recognizing the limits of personal troubleshooting and utilizing the wealth of resources and expertise available through Apple Support and the wider tech community. This approach ensures that your iPad remains a reliable, effective tool in your digital arsenal, backed by a network of support and knowledge.

Chapter 11. iPad Security and Privacy

Embarking on the journey of iPad Security and Privacy is an essential aspect of owning and operating this powerful device. In a world where digital security threats loom large, understanding how to protect your personal information and maintain privacy on your iPad is not just a precaution; it's a necessity. This chapter delves into the critical aspects of digital defense, from comprehending and configuring privacy settings to the intricacies of safeguarding personal data. We explore the importance of safe browsing habits, the pivotal role of passcodes, and strategies to ward off scams and phishing attempts. Each section is crafted to empower you with knowledge and tools, ensuring that your experience with your iPad is both secure and enjoyable. It's about creating a digital environment where you can explore, work, and connect with peace of mind, knowing that your data and privacy are well-protected.

Understanding Privacy Settings

In an era where digital privacy is as vital as personal security, understanding and configuring the privacy settings on your iPad is akin to setting up a personalized security system for your digital home. This process is not just about toggling switches or selecting options; it's a proactive approach to safeguarding your personal information and digital footprint. The privacy settings on your iPad serve as gatekeepers, allowing you to control what information is shared and with whom, making it an essential aspect of responsible and secure device usage.

The journey of navigating through privacy settings begins with an exploration of what these settings control. Each setting is a guardian of a specific aspect of your digital privacy. Location services, for instance, determine which apps have access to your geographical location. It's akin to deciding who gets a key to the front door of your house. By managing these settings, you can ensure that only trusted apps can access your location, and only when absolutely necessary.

Another critical aspect is the management of app permissions. Each app on your iPad requests access to certain features or data, such as your camera, microphone, or contacts. Understanding and managing these permissions is like vetting guests in your home; you decide who gets access to what. This control helps prevent sensitive information from falling into the wrong hands or being used without your consent.

Privacy settings also extend to the way your personal data is handled and shared. The iPad offers options to limit ad tracking, control how your data is shared with Apple, and decide whether your usage data is used to improve Apple products. These settings are akin to setting boundaries in a relationship; they allow you to decide how much or how little you want to share, fostering a sense of control and comfort in your digital interactions.

The Safari browser on your iPad also comes with a range of privacy-enhancing features. These include preventing cross-site tracking, blocking all cookies, and private browsing mode. Navigating these settings is similar to choosing the right curtains and blinds for your home's windows; they determine how much of your online activity is visible to outside observers, such as advertisers and websites.

In addition to these settings, understanding how to review and manage the information you share with iCloud is crucial. iCloud stores a wealth of personal data, from photos and documents to contacts and notes. Ensuring that your iCloud settings align with your privacy preferences is akin to securing a personal safe; it's about making sure that your most precious digital assets are well-protected yet accessible when you need them.

Furthermore, Apple continuously updates the iPad's operating system with new privacy features and enhancements. Keeping your device updated is like upgrading your home's security system; it ensures that you are equipped with the latest tools to protect your privacy.

In essence, understanding and configuring the privacy settings on your iPad is a fundamental step in protecting your digital persona. It's about making informed decisions regarding the accessibility of your personal information and maintaining control over your digital presence. As you delve into and customize these settings, your iPad becomes more than just a device; it becomes a trusted companion that respects and protects your privacy, offering peace of mind in an increasingly connected world.

Protecting Personal Information

In the digital age, where personal information is as valuable as physical assets, safeguarding this data on your iPad becomes a critical responsibility. Protecting personal information is not just a defensive maneuver against potential threats; it's a proactive approach to maintaining your digital autonomy and safety. Your iPad, a repository of personal details, communications, and documents, should be fortified like a digital fortress, impervious to unwarranted access and breaches.

The first step in this process is understanding the scope of personal information stored on your iPad. This information can range from your contact details and emails to sensitive financial data and personal photographs. Each of these pieces of information is akin to a valuable item stored in your home, deserving of protection and care. Acknowledging the value of this data is crucial in motivating the necessary steps to safeguard it.

One of the most effective methods of protecting personal information is through the use of strong, unique passwords for your Apple ID and other accounts accessed via your iPad. These passwords act as the first line of defense, akin to a robust lock on your front door, preventing unauthorized access to your digital domain. Utilizing a combination of letters, numbers, and symbols in your passwords, and avoiding common words and phrases, significantly bolsters this defense.

In addition to strong passwords, enabling two-factor authentication (2FA) for your Apple ID and other critical accounts adds an extra layer of security. This process is like having a security system in your home that requires a second form of verification, ensuring that only you can gain access, even if someone else knows your password. With 2FA, a code is sent to a trusted device or phone number, which must be entered along with your password to access your account.

Being mindful of the apps you install and the permissions you grant them is another vital aspect of protecting your personal information. Each app on your iPad should be treated like a guest in your home; their access should be scrutinized and limited to what is necessary for them to function. Regularly reviewing app permissions and uninstalling apps that are no longer needed or seem suspicious can prevent these digital guests from overstepping their boundaries.

The importance of regularly backing up your iPad cannot be overstated. In the unfortunate event of data loss or device theft, having a backup ensures that your personal information is not lost forever. It's akin to having insurance for your valuables, providing a safety net in times of need. Backups can be done via iCloud or your computer, giving you options to secure your data in a way that best suits your needs.

Moreover, being cautious about public Wi-Fi networks is crucial. These networks can be breeding grounds for data interception and theft. When using public Wi-Fi, avoid accessing sensitive information or conducting financial transactions. It's similar to being cautious in unfamiliar or crowded places; you would safeguard your wallet, and similarly, you should safeguard your digital information.

Lastly, staying informed about the latest security threats and how to counter them is key. Just as you would stay informed about safety issues in your neighborhood, keeping abreast of digital security trends helps you prepare and respond effectively to potential threats.

So, protecting personal information on your iPad requires a combination of strong security practices, regular maintenance of your digital accounts, and a vigilant attitude towards potential threats. By treating your digital data with the same care and seriousness as your physical valuables, you can significantly mitigate the risk of unauthorized access and data breaches, ensuring your personal information remains secure in the digital realm.

Safe Browsing Practices

Navigating the vast digital landscape of the internet on your iPad requires not only a sense of exploration but also a commitment to safe browsing practices. These practices are not mere precautions; they are essential habits that safeguard your digital well-being in an online world brimming with potential threats. Safe browsing on your iPad is akin to traveling through unknown territories with a reliable map and a set of guidelines to avoid pitfalls and dangers.

Understanding the importance of safe browsing begins with recognizing the internet as a double-edged sword – it offers a wealth of information and connectivity but also harbors risks like malware, identity theft, and phishing scams. Your iPad, while equipped with advanced security features, still relies on your informed decisions and actions to ensure a secure browsing experience. It's similar to driving a car with advanced safety features; the technology provides protection, but the driver's awareness and choices are paramount.

The first principle of safe browsing is staying vigilant about the websites you visit. Just as you would avoid walking down a dangerous alley, you should steer clear of suspicious or unfamiliar websites. These sites may harbor malware that can infect your device, steal personal information, or compromise your privacy. Always look for signs of website security, such as a URL that begins with 'https' and a padlock icon in the address bar. These symbols are akin to seeing a safety certification on a physical product; they indicate that the website is taking measures to secure your data.

Using strong and unique passwords for online accounts is another cornerstone of safe browsing. Each online account should have a distinct password, much like having a different key for every lock. This practice prevents a breach in one account from cascading into unauthorized access to all your accounts. Consider using a password manager, which acts like a secure vault, keeping your passwords safe and easily accessible only to you.

Enabling two-factor authentication (2FA) wherever possible adds an extra layer of security to your online activities. This method is like having a double-lock system; even if someone obtains your password, they still need a second piece of information – usually a code sent to your phone or email – to access your account. It significantly reduces the risk of unauthorized access.

Being cautious with personal information while browsing is critical. Be wary of sharing sensitive information such as your address, phone number, or financial details, especially on websites that do not show clear signs of security. It's akin to not sharing personal details with strangers in public places. Additionally, be mindful of the information you share on social media, as oversharing can make you a target for identity theft or scams.

Regularly updating your iPad's software, including the browser, plays a crucial role in safe browsing. These updates often include patches for security vulnerabilities that have been identified. Ignoring software updates is like neglecting to maintain safety equipment; it can leave you exposed to avoidable risks.

Moreover, installing and using reputable security apps and ad blockers can enhance your browsing safety. These tools act as sentinels, guarding against intrusive ads and tracking, and protecting against malicious content. It's important, however, to choose these tools wisely, as some can be counterproductive, masquerading as security apps while being harmful themselves.

Finally, staying informed about the latest online threats and scams is essential. The landscape of cyber threats is constantly evolving, and staying updated is akin to keeping abreast of news about road closures or hazards in the context of a physical journey. Awareness is a powerful tool in the realm of digital security.

So, safe browsing practices on your iPad are vital in the modern digital age. These practices involve being cautious about where you browse, how you manage your online presence, and how you protect your personal information. By adopting a proactive and knowledgeable approach to online safety, you empower yourself to explore the digital world securely, making your iPad a trusted companion in your digital adventures.

Setting Up and Using Passcodes

In the digital age, securing your iPad with a passcode is akin to placing a robust lock on the door of your personal data vault. This security measure goes beyond a mere four-digit code; it represents a fundamental layer of defense against unauthorized access to your private information and applications. Setting up and using passcodes on your iPad is not just a technical procedure; it's a commitment to safeguarding your digital identity, akin to protecting the keys to your home.

Understanding the importance of a passcode on your iPad begins with recognizing the wealth of personal data your device holds. From emails and messages to photos and documents, your iPad is a treasure trove of personal and often sensitive information. A passcode acts as the first line of defense, much like a gatekeeper, ensuring that only you or trusted individuals gain access. This digital barrier is crucial in today's world, where information security breaches are not just nuisances but serious threats.

Setting up a passcode on your iPad is a straightforward yet vital process. It involves selecting a unique code that is easy for you to remember but challenging for others to guess. While a simple four-digit code offers a basic level of security, opting for a longer passcode with a mix of numbers, letters, and special characters significantly enhances security. This step is akin to choosing a complex combination for a safe; the more intricate it is, the tougher it is for intruders to crack.

In addition to setting a strong passcode, the frequency and conditions under which it is required play a crucial role in security. Configuring your iPad to require the passcode immediately after sleep or screen timeout adds an additional layer of security. This setting ensures that your device is not left unprotected, similar to never leaving your front door unlocked when you step out, even for a brief moment.

The Touch ID and Face ID features on newer iPad models further augment security with biometric authentication. These technologies use your fingerprint or facial recognition as a passcode, offering a more personalized and often more secure method of locking and unlocking your device. Using biometric authentication is like having a high-tech security system that recognizes only you and denies entry to anyone else.

Regularly updating your passcode is also an essential practice. Just as you might periodically change the locks or security codes in your physical environment, updating your digital passcode helps mitigate risks associated with potential code leakage or guessing. It's a simple yet effective habit that maintains the robustness of your iPad's security over time.

In scenarios where you might forget your passcode, Apple provides recovery options to regain access to your device. However, this process can be time-consuming and may result in data loss if backups are not available. Therefore, keeping a record of your passcode in a secure and retrievable manner, much like storing a spare key in a safe place, is advisable.

In essence, setting up and using passcodes on your iPad is a critical aspect of your digital security strategy. It's a practice that balances ease of access with the necessity of protecting personal and sensitive data. By conscientiously selecting, using, and managing passcodes, you fortify your iPad against unauthorized access, ensuring that your private information remains just that – private. In the digital world, where security threats are ever-present and evolving, a robust passcode system on your iPad is not just a recommendation; it's an imperative.

Avoiding Scams and Phishing

In the vast expanse of the digital world, scams and phishing attempts are akin to hidden traps on a treacherous path. These deceptive tactics, designed to steal your personal and financial information, pose a significant threat to users navigating the internet on their iPads. Understanding and avoiding these scams is not just about being cautious; it's about being equipped with the knowledge and tools to recognize and evade these digital pitfalls. This defensive strategy is crucial in maintaining the sanctity and security of your personal data in an environment rife with cyber threats.

Phishing scams, in particular, are insidious because they masquerade as legitimate requests or notifications. These scams can arrive in various forms, such as emails, text messages, or even through websites, attempting to lure you into providing sensitive information like passwords, credit card numbers, or social security numbers. The trickery involved in phishing is comparable to a wolf in sheep's clothing; it looks harmless, even familiar, but harbors malicious intent.

The first step in avoiding these scams is developing a keen eye for recognizing them. Phishing attempts often contain tell-tale signs such as urgent or threatening language, requests for immediate action, misspellings, or unfamiliar email addresses. It's akin to spotting a disguised intruder; knowing what to look for is half the battle. Always be skeptical of unsolicited requests for personal information, no matter how urgent they seem. Legitimate organizations, especially banks and government agencies, will never ask for sensitive information through such informal channels.

Another crucial practice is verifying the authenticity of the communication. If you receive an email or message that appears to be from a reputable source but asks for personal information, take the time to verify it. This verification can be as simple as contacting the organization directly through official channels. It's like double-checking the identity of a visitor before opening your door. This step is crucial because scammers often create a sense of urgency to prompt a hasty response.

Enhancing the security settings on your iPad can also provide a robust defense against scams. Utilize features like fraud warning in Safari, which can alert you to suspicious websites, and be cautious about the permissions you grant to apps and websites. It's akin to installing a security system in your home; it provides an additional layer of defense against intruders.

Be wary of clicking on links or downloading attachments from unknown sources. These actions can be compared to opening a mysterious package left at your doorstep. They can lead to malicious sites or download malware onto your device. Instead, navigate to websites by typing the URL directly into the browser or using bookmarks.

Educating yourself about the latest scamming and phishing techniques is also essential. Scammers continually evolve their tactics, so staying informed about new methods of deception is like keeping up with the latest security measures for your home or personal safety.

Lastly, in the unfortunate event that you fall victim to a scam, act swiftly. Contact your bank to secure your accounts, change your passwords, and report the incident to the appropriate authorities. Taking immediate action can mitigate the damage and prevent further loss.

In conclusion, avoiding scams and phishing attempts while using your iPad requires vigilance, awareness, and proactive security measures. By understanding the nature of these threats, recognizing the signs, and taking the necessary precautions, you can navigate the digital world with confidence, keeping your personal information safe from the clutches of cyber predators. In a world where digital interactions are increasingly intertwined with our daily lives, cultivating these safe practices is not just advisable; it is imperative for your online security and privacy.

Chapter 12. Living with iPad: Integrating into Your Lifestyle

Embracing the iPad as a versatile partner in your daily life opens a world of possibilities that seamlessly blend technology with your personal and social routines. This chapter delves into the multifaceted ways the iPad can enrich various aspects of your lifestyle. From transforming your culinary experiences in the kitchen and enhancing your creative hobbies and crafts, to being an indispensable companion during your travels, the iPad proves to be remarkably adaptable. It extends its utility to being a pivotal tool in maintaining fitness and health, and perhaps most importantly, acts as a bridge for staying connected with family and community. Each section is crafted to explore how the iPad can be integrated into these significant areas of life, offering practical insights and creative ways to make the most of this dynamic device. The iPad thus becomes more than a gadget; it becomes an integral part of your daily narrative, enriching your experiences and connections.

iPad for Cooking and Recipes

Incorporating the iPad into your kitchen adventures transforms the way you cook and interact with recipes, merging the art of cooking with the convenience of technology. The iPad, in this culinary context, becomes more than just a device; it emerges as a dynamic, interactive cookbook and a versatile kitchen assistant. This integration of technology into cooking is not just about having digital recipes at your fingertips; it's about enhancing your entire culinary experience, from planning meals to executing complex dishes.

The journey of using the iPad in your culinary endeavors begins with the exploration of an array of apps dedicated to cooking and recipes. These apps serve as gateways to a world of diverse cuisines, techniques, and flavors, akin to having an international team of chefs guiding you. Whether you are a novice cook or a seasoned chef, these apps offer tailored experiences, featuring step-by-step cooking guides, video tutorials, and customizable recipes. It's like enrolling in a digital culinary school, where learning and experimenting with new dishes become a daily adventure.

One of the standout features of using an iPad for cooking is the ease of accessing and organizing recipes. You can store your favorite recipes in one place, create weekly meal plans, and even generate shopping lists based on the ingredients required for your chosen dishes. This organization transforms meal planning from a tedious task into a streamlined, enjoyable process. It's akin to having a personal sous-chef who helps you plan and prepare for every meal.

Moreover, the interactive nature of the iPad adds a new dimension to following recipes. Touchscreen functionality allows you to easily navigate through recipes, zoom in on tricky steps, and even set timers for different cooking stages. This interaction is like having a responsive cooking guide that adapts to your pace and style, making the cooking process more intuitive and engaging.

For those who love to share their culinary creations, the iPad doubles as a tool for social engagement. You can take photos of your dishes, share recipes with friends and family, or even live stream your cooking sessions. This connectivity turns cooking into a shared experience, breaking down the barriers of physical distance. It's like hosting a virtual dinner party, where your kitchen becomes a stage to showcase your culinary skills and connect with fellow food enthusiasts.

The iPad also offers an array of tools and resources for health-conscious cooks. With apps focused on nutritional information, dietary restrictions, and healthy cooking, the iPad supports a lifestyle that values wellness and informed food choices. It's like having a nutritionist and health coach right in your kitchen, guiding you towards healthier eating habits.

In essence, using the iPad for cooking and recipes is about more than just convenience; it's about enriching your cooking experience. The iPad becomes a bridge that connects the traditional art of cooking with the modern world of technology, offering tools, resources, and connectivity that elevate your culinary skills. It's about transforming your kitchen into a place of exploration, learning, and sharing, making every meal an opportunity to discover and delight in the joys of cooking.

Using iPad for Hobbies and Crafts

In the realm of hobbies and crafts, the iPad emerges as a versatile tool that enriches and expands the boundaries of creative expression. Integrating the iPad into your artistic and crafty pursuits is not just about digitizing these activities; it's about opening a gateway to a world of endless possibilities, inspiration, and convenience. The iPad, in this context, becomes more than a tablet; it transforms into an artist's canvas, a designer's sketchbook, a crafter's companion, and a source of boundless creative resources.

Imagine stepping into a room filled with the finest art supplies, instructional books, and inspirational guides. That's the experience the iPad offers to hobbyists and craft enthusiasts. With an array of apps designed for drawing, painting, designing, knitting, and more, the iPad serves as a digital studio where creativity knows no bounds. These apps provide tools and features that replicate the experience of using physical art supplies, from textured brushes to color palettes, while also offering the advantages of digital art, such as undo options and layers.

For artists, the iPad's compatibility with styluses like the Apple Pencil elevates the drawing and painting experience. The precision and pressure sensitivity of these tools allow for fine details and nuanced artistry that rivals traditional mediums. Whether you're sketching landscapes, designing characters, or painting digital portraits, the iPad offers a portable, clean, and versatile environment to unleash your creativity. It's like having an entire art studio at your fingertips, ready whenever inspiration strikes.

Crafters and DIY enthusiasts also find a treasure trove of resources in the iPad. From instructional videos and step-by-step tutorials to pattern libraries and design tools, the iPad is a central hub for crafting ideas and guidance. You can explore new crafting techniques, find templates and patterns, or even create your own designs directly on the device. The iPad becomes a crafting companion that not only stores your ideas but also inspires new ones.

Beyond the creation process, the iPad plays a pivotal role in learning and honing your craft. Various apps offer courses, tutorials, and workshops in different creative fields. You can learn to play a musical instrument, start a home DIY project, or dive into the intricacies of photography, all through interactive and engaging lessons tailored to your pace and skill level. This aspect of the iPad is like having a personal tutor, guiding you through each step of your learning journey.

Moreover, the iPad serves as a platform for sharing your creations and connecting with like-minded individuals. You can showcase your artwork, crafts, or DIY projects on social media platforms and forums, receive feedback, and engage with a community of enthusiasts and professionals. This connectivity brings a sense of belonging and motivation, as you become part of a global network of creators sharing their passions and inspirations.

The iPad's portability further enhances its role in hobbies and crafts. Whether you're capturing nature's beauty on a plein air painting app, designing a quilt pattern while relaxing in your living room, or taking online photography classes in a café, the iPad adapts to your lifestyle and location. It's like carrying a portable workshop or studio wherever you go, making it easy to stay engaged with your hobbies no matter your setting.

In essence, integrating the iPad into your hobbies and crafts is about embracing a digital dimension that complements and enhances your artistic and creative pursuits. It opens up new avenues for exploration, learning, and sharing, bridging the gap between traditional crafting methods and the digital revolution. The iPad, in this light, is not just a tool; it's a partner in your creative journey, enabling you to explore, create, and connect in ways that were once unimaginable.

Traveling with Your iPad

Embracing the iPad as a travel companion is akin to carrying a multifaceted digital Swiss Army knife on your journeys. Integrating the iPad into your travel experiences transcends its use as a mere entertainment device; it becomes a navigator, a guide, a storyteller, and a connector, all housed within a sleek, portable screen. This integration is not just about convenience; it's about enriching your travel experiences, making every trip more manageable, enjoyable, and memorable.

The iPad's role in travel begins even before you set foot outside your door. Planning and organizing your trip can be a complex task, but with the iPad, it becomes a seamless experience. Travel apps provide comprehensive tools for booking flights, reserving accommodations, and creating itineraries. It's like having a personal travel agent at your fingertips, helping you craft the perfect trip tailored to your preferences. You can explore destinations through immersive content, read reviews from fellow travelers, and even secure tickets to attractions and events, all from the comfort of your home.

Once you embark on your journey, the iPad serves as an invaluable guide and assistant. With its robust mapping and navigation capabilities, it helps you explore new places with confidence. Whether you're navigating the labyrinthine streets of an ancient city or finding your way through sprawling airports, the iPad ensures you're never truly lost. Its ability to download maps for offline use is particularly useful in areas with limited internet access, akin to having a trusty map in your backpack.

The iPad also transforms into your personal entertainment hub during travel. Long flights, train rides, or waiting periods become opportunities to dive into your favorite books, movies, shows, or games. With its high-resolution display and long battery life, the iPad provides a premium viewing and gaming experience. It's like carrying a portable cinema and library, ensuring that downtime during your travels is never dull.

For those who love to document their travels, the iPad is a powerful tool. With its camera capabilities and a suite of photo and video editing apps, you can capture and edit stunning images and videos on the go. The iPad becomes a digital canvas where you can chronicle your adventures, create travel vlogs, or compose beautiful photographs, turning your memories into visual stories.

In addition, the iPad is a bridge that keeps you connected to your work, family, and friends while traveling. With video conferencing apps, email, and messaging services, staying in touch with your personal and professional life is effortless. This connectivity ensures that you're never too far away, whether you're attending a virtual meeting from a beachside café or sharing your travel experiences with loved ones through a video call.

The iPad also serves as a fitness companion during your travels. With health and fitness apps, you can maintain your workout routine, track your activities, or even meditate to rejuvenate after a long day of exploration. It's like having a personal trainer and wellness coach accompanying you, helping you stay active and balanced.

In essence, traveling with your iPad is about harnessing the power of technology to elevate your travel experiences. From planning and exploring to capturing and sharing your adventures, the iPad enriches every aspect of your journey. It's a testament to how technology can complement the human experience of travel, making every trip more organized, entertaining, connected, and memorable. With your iPad in tow, the world is not just at your fingertips; it's an open book waiting to be explored and experienced.

iPad for Fitness and Health Tracking

Integrating the iPad into your fitness and health routine is akin to having a personal trainer, nutritionist, and wellness coach all rolled into one sleek, digital package. This integration is not merely about tracking calories or steps; it's a holistic approach to managing and enhancing your overall health and well-being. The iPad, with its array of health and fitness applications, becomes a central hub for your wellness journey, offering tools and insights that cater to your unique health goals and lifestyle.

The journey of using the iPad for fitness and health tracking starts with understanding the myriad of apps available at your fingertips. These apps range from workout guides and fitness trackers to meditation aids and sleep monitors. Each app serves a specific purpose, functioning like a piece of equipment in a gym; together, they create a comprehensive fitness and wellness toolkit tailored to your needs. Whether you're aiming to lose weight, build muscle, improve flexibility, or simply maintain a healthy lifestyle, there's an app to guide you on that path.

Workout and exercise apps transform your iPad into a virtual gym. With a variety of workout routines, instructional videos, and personalized training programs, these apps provide the guidance and motivation akin to a personal trainer. Whether you prefer yoga, strength training, cardio, or pilates, you can find routines to match your fitness level and preferences. The interactive nature of these apps allows you to track your progress, set goals, and gradually increase the intensity of your workouts, ensuring a balanced and effective fitness regimen.

Nutrition and diet apps are equally crucial in your health tracking arsenal. These apps function like a digital dietitian, helping you monitor your food intake, balance your macronutrients, and stay on track with your dietary goals. With features like barcode scanning, meal logging, and calorie counting, you maintain a detailed record of your eating habits. Moreover, many apps provide healthy recipes and nutrition tips, making it easier to adopt and stick to a nutritious diet.

Sleep tracking apps offer insights into your sleep patterns, an often-overlooked aspect of health and wellness. By analyzing your sleep quality and duration, these apps help you understand the factors affecting your sleep and offer tips to improve it. Good sleep is foundational to overall health, and by using these apps, you effectively give your body the rest it needs to recover and rejuvenate.

For mindfulness and mental well-being, the iPad offers a range of meditation and relaxation apps. These apps guide you through meditation exercises, breathing techniques, and mindfulness practices, aiding in stress reduction and mental clarity. It's like having a serene sanctuary within your device, where you can take a few moments to unwind and center yourself, regardless of your surroundings.

Moreover, the integration of the iPad with wearable technology like the Apple Watch further enhances its capabilities as a health and fitness tool. This synchronization allows for real-time health data monitoring, from heart rate tracking to activity levels, providing a comprehensive view of your physical health.

In essence, the iPad as a tool for fitness and health tracking is about embracing technology to support and enrich your wellness journey. It provides a personalized, interactive, and holistic approach to health management, making it easier to achieve and maintain your health and fitness goals. In a world where health is wealth, the iPad becomes an invaluable asset in your pursuit of a healthier, happier lifestyle.

Staying Connected with Family and Community

In a world where the pace of life accelerates daily, the iPad emerges as a beacon of connectivity, bridging distances and bringing people closer. Integrating the iPad into your lifestyle for staying connected with family and community is about more than just communication; it's about nurturing relationships, sharing experiences, and being present in each other's lives, regardless of physical distances. The iPad, in this role, transcends its status as a mere device; it becomes a window to loved ones, a platform for community engagement, and a tool for sustaining bonds that matter the most.

The iPad's capability to connect with family is akin to having a magical portal. Video calling apps like FaceTime transform the screen into a vibrant canvas where faces of loved ones come alive, making conversations more personal and engaging. Whether it's a routine check-in with parents, reading a bedtime story to a grandchild, or sharing a meal with a distant relative, these interactions foster a sense of closeness and intimacy. The iPad thus breaks down the barriers of distance, ensuring that miles apart doesn't mean out of touch.

For families spread across the globe, the iPad serves as a digital gathering place. Through group chats, shared photo albums, and collaborative apps, it creates a virtual family room where memories are shared, plans are made, and life's milestones are celebrated. Organizing a family reunion, planning a holiday, or just sharing the day's happenings becomes effortless and inclusive, keeping the family fabric tightly woven.

In the realm of community engagement, the iPad proves to be an invaluable asset. It offers access to local community groups, forums, and social platforms where communal activities, local events, and volunteer opportunities are shared. For seniors or individuals with mobility issues, the iPad is a lifeline to community interaction, enabling participation in group discussions, access to community services, and engagement with local news and events. It's like having a community center at your fingertips, where involvement is just a few taps away.

The iPad also serves as a bridge for cultural exchange and learning. With access to a vast array of online courses, webinars, and workshops, you can explore new cultures, learn languages, or delve into the history and traditions of various communities. This learning not only enriches your knowledge but also empowers you to connect with people from diverse backgrounds, fostering understanding and empathy.

For those with shared interests or hobbies, the iPad is a tool for finding and connecting with like-minded individuals. Whether it's gardening, photography, literature, or technology, there are numerous groups and forums where ideas and experiences are exchanged. This connectivity not only enhances your hobbies but also builds a sense of belonging and camaraderie, creating a community of shared passions and interests.

Lastly, in a world where keeping up with family news and staying informed about community issues is increasingly challenging, the iPad brings a sense of order and accessibility. Customizable news apps and notifications ensure that you stay updated on the matters closest to your heart, whether it's your niece's graduation or a local charity event.

In conclusion, integrating the iPad into your lifestyle for staying connected with family and community is about harnessing technology to enrich your personal and communal relationships. It's a testament to how a device can be much more than a tool for communication – it can be a catalyst for nurturing relationships, building communities, and keeping the warmth of human connections alive in a digital age. With the iPad, you remain an integral part of your family's tapestry and an active participant in your community, no matter where life takes you.

The journey through the diverse ways of integrating the iPad into your lifestyle highlights its role as an invaluable extension of your daily activities. Whether it's adding flavor to your cooking ventures, bringing creativity to your hobbies, accompanying you on travels, aiding in your health and fitness goals, or keeping you connected with loved ones, the iPad has demonstrated its versatility and adaptability. This exploration reveals that the iPad is not just about technological interaction but about enhancing the quality of life, making tasks more enjoyable, and relationships more profound. It stands as a testament to how technology can be thoughtfully woven into the fabric of our lives, not as a distraction, but as an enabler of richer experiences and deeper connections. Ultimately, this chapter isn't just a guide to using a device; it's about embracing a lifestyle where technology and personal life harmonize, creating a symphony of efficiency, creativity, wellness, and connectivity.

Made in the USA
Las Vegas, NV
03 January 2025

15761980R00090